Date Due

MINIATURES

AND

SILHOUETTES

Holbein.   *Portrait of Man with a Lily*

MINIATURES
AND
SILHOUETTES

BY

MAX VON BOEHN

TRANSLATED BY

E. K. WALKER

BENJAMIN BLOM
New York

First Published London, 1928
Reissued 1970 by
Benjamin Blom, Inc., New York 10025

Library of Congress Catalog Card Number 70-145772

Printed in the United States of America

PUBLISHER'S NOTE

THE reproductions of the two Hilliard miniatures of Lady Jane Grey and Queen Elizabeth (Nos. 6 and 7) are included by gracious permission, now gratefully acknowledged, of His Majesty the King.

We are indebted to Dr. G. C. Williamson, the well-known English authority on miniatures, in the first place for pointing out to us that a number of the illustrations to *Miniaturen und Silhouetten*, Munich, 1917 (of which the present volume is a translation), were likely to infringe copyrights if published in England; and in the second place for the loan of many photographs, notably those numbered 8, 10, 11, 22, 27, 28, 29, 30, 32, 33, 34, 35, 36, 38, 46, 47, 66, 90 and 133, which we have been able to substitute, by Dr. Williamson's permission, for the original copyright illustrations. Students desiring a wider acquaintance with miniatures and their history cannot do better than make use of Dr. Williamson's many works on the subject.

We desire also to record our obligation to the executors of the late J. J. Foster, F.S.A., author of *British Miniature Painters and their Works*, *Miniature Painters: British and Foreign*, *A Dictionary of Painters of Miniatures*, and other standard works on portraiture, for permission to use the reproductions numbered 15, 16, 20, 21, 23, 31, 50, 58 and 102; and to Messrs. Macmillan and Company Ltd., for leave to include those numbered 17 and 52, from *A History of Miniature Art* by J. L. Propert.

Our thanks are due likewise to Messrs. Geo. Bell & Sons

Ltd. for their kindness in lending us the original blocks for items 8, 22, 27, 28, 32 and 35.

The illustrations numbered 9, 14, 41, 42, 57, 77, 85, 114 and 115, have been reproduced from *L'Exposition de la Miniature à Bruxelles*, 1912, by kind permission of the publisher; and Plate XIII. (opposite p. 59) is taken, by permission, from an illustration made for *La Miniature Française* by M. Bouchot before the original passed into the collection of which it now forms part.

CONTENTS

In the original edition the following plates were reproduced in color; in this edition they appear in black and white.

LIST OF COLOURED ILLUSTRATIONS

No. 1.   Holbein.   *Portrait of Himself*

THE MINIATURE AND ITS HISTORY

TECHNIQUE

A MINIATURE is a painting, primarily a portrait, of small, often minute, dimensions. The name is associated with the book illustration of the Middle Ages; *miniator* was the title given to the scribe whose duty it was to illuminate with the red colour *"minium"* the capital letters and chapter-headings of the manuscript. This employment gradually developed into the art of miniature-painting in body-colour and gold, an art which reached its zenith in the fifteenth century. In the early mediæval manuscripts there are representations which may possibly be intended for portraits; these are mostly in the dedicatory pages—scenes in which the author is depicted offering his work to some prince or princess. Though the greatest care is bestowed on details of costume and ornament, it is more than doubtful whether we may regard the faces as portraits of the actors in the scene.

No. 2. Clovio. *Portrait of Himself*

The true portrait does not make its appearance until the end of the Middle Ages, at the moment when the Renaissance

3

No. 3.   Holbein.   *Henry VIII.*

awakened men to a sense of the personal and individual. Until then each man had been submerged in the mass, and his individuality enslaved by the state, the township and the church. He could only express himself or have any importance when linked with like-minded men in corporations, guilds, orders and brotherhoods. In such conditions no interest in portraits could be expected, and therefore it was not until the Renaissance taught men to seek human greatness in highly developed personalities

rather than in the mass, that the portrait flourished, and proved that features and bearing were also essential and important assets of greatness. The great Early Renaissance painters of Italy were the first to create really faithful portraits of their contemporaries, both in frescoes and easel-pictures.

In book illustration the portrait appears much later. Jean Clouet (1485–1544) is the earliest artist whose creations can truly be claimed as likenesses. He was a painter of the French court, and, in the Bibliothèque Nationale, in a manuscript of

No. 4.   Holbein.   *Anne of Cleves*

"*Commentaires de la guerre gallique,*" there are portraits by him, no larger than a five-franc piece, of various courtiers. The British Museum, the collection of the Duke of Aumâle at Chantilly, and several other libraries, contain similar works by him.

The small portrait was now an accomplished fact; it only needed to be dissociated from the book and framed, or applied as some form of ornament, to become a miniature in the modern sense. This step was taken, according to Henri Bouchot, at the time of King Charles VIII.'s romantic and famous expedition over the Alps. His knights, who were to be parted from the ladies of their hearts for many a long day, perhaps for ever, left portraits of themselves with their mistresses, and bore off those of the ladies in exchange.

No. 5. Holbein.
Unknown Lady

Though this romantic conjecture may be right, nothing remains to substantiate this claim, since the earliest single miniatures we know of do not date back farther than the middle of the sixteenth century. At any rate, the book illuminators were some time considering the matter before they took up miniature portrait-painting, and single likenesses, even by famous masters of the craft, are extremely rare. The collection of the Imperial family in Vienna contains one such in the self-portrait of Giulio Clovio (1498–1578).

This famous illuminator was a Croat by birth, and his name was spelt Giorgio Glovicié; but in the sixteenth century people Italianised their names instead of making them Slavonic, as is the fashion nowadays, and so he called himself Giulio Clovio, to demonstrate his allegiance to an ancient civilisation. Though this artist is unsurpassed by any of his contemporaries in technical skill, he must be denied creative originality, for he borrowed from Raphael and Michelangelo. His taste also leaves a great deal to be desired, for he was fond of loading his compositions with ornaments. Just as Benvenuto Cellini was credited with every article worked in rare metals, so all the better miniature-work was ascribed to Giulio Clovio; but only a few of the best pieces now hold their ground against severe criticism. The artist lived for the most part in Rome, and died in the Palazzo Farnese. El Greco has painted him with one of his masterpieces in his hand.

The art of the small single likeness, or miniature, was approached from two directions. On the one hand, the painter tended to cut down the size of his picture more and more, and to use finer brushes for his work, and, on the other hand, the book illuminator frequently kept his portrait independent of the text and isolated it by a border or frame.

No. 6.   Hilliard.   *Lady Jane Grey*

The technique of the miniature shows this twofold origin. Many miniatures of the sixteenth and seventeenth centuries were carried out in oils on sheets of copper, silver, slate or even gold, and were the work of great artists. The majority of miniaturists, however, preferred gouache or water-colours to oils, which are ill-suited to this purpose. They usually chose vellum or card to paint on, whilst Holbein and some of his school liked to use the backs of playing-cards. In this method of procedure the ground is left and serves the artist as a tone for the face and hands, all the rest being covered with rows of minute strokes and dots.

Towards the end of the seventeenth century a great advance was made by the use of ivory as a foundation. It is

Cosway.   *George III*

Engleheart.   *George IV*

true that Lemberger mentions a painting on ivory of the Duchess Dorothea Ursula of Württemberg, in 1577, as the earliest German miniature on this material, but it is quite exceptional. Ivory did not attain any importance for this purpose until a hundred years later. No sooner was it employed than it displaced all other materials; its advantage over

No. 7. Hilliard. *Queen Elizabeth*

vellum or paper was seen to consist in the delicate and natural transparency which it imparts to the flesh-colour. On ivory the complexion acquires a warmth and delicacy, a glow of life, which no other foundation can produce; paper always gives a chalky effect, vellum tends to look yellowish.

After the use of ivory became general the technique made rapid strides. By the middle of the eighteenth century the French miniaturists had seventeen or eighteen different shades of flesh-tones, and Jean Baptiste Jacques Augustin (1759–1832) raised this number to twenty-five different tints. In Paris, at the time of Louis XV., miniature-painters could actually buy their colours all ready prepared in shops, whilst painters in oils were still obliged to prepare their colours themselves. Tinfoil was sometimes laid under the ivory to increase its transparency and show up the colour, but in course of time oxidisation has produced precisely the opposite effect, and the colouring now appears muddy and dull.

Artists vied with one another in the invention of all manner of little tricks wherewith to impart fresh charms to their productions and by new combinations of material, colour and decoration to create novel and astonishing effects. Armand Vincent de Montpetit (*d.* 1800) invented what is known as *eludoric* painting. It is executed in oil on linen or taffeta, and pasted on to the underside of glass. This method, which reminds us somewhat of the art of painting under glass or *eglomisé*, was used by Genillon, Martin Drolling and Gérard von Spaendonck, in addition to the inventor himself. August Grahl (1791–1868) employed oils on ivory, and was never tired of experimenting in the technique of his art. He almost seemed to prefer the study of the means to the practice of painting itself, but, as he wrote nothing down, all his discoveries were lost to us at his death.

No. 8. Cosway
Richard Cosway in old age
Olim Hodgkins Collection

In the seventeenth century there flourished in England, side by side with miniature-painting, an art known as Plumbago; the portrait was carried out with pencil. Miniatures in pen and ink were frequently met with in Germany at this time, and at the end of the century a certain Johann Michel of Augsburg excelled in portraits in which the hair and dress were done in handwriting; the text being generally a life-history of the person represented. Conceits of this kind were very popular. For instance, Hans Wechter did a portrait of King Christian IV. of Denmark at Erfurt, in 1640, in minute writing, for which he drew from the twelve chapters of Ecclesiastes, the twenty-fifth chapter of the Proverbs of Solomon, the fifth chapter of the book of Wisdom and the third chapter of the first book of Kings.

There were similar extravagances of various kinds, and Lemberger tells of needle-work portraits of the second half of the eighteenth century, in which Caroline Friederike Schlözer of

No. 9. Anon. English XVI. Century
Mary Tudor, Queen of England
Collection Baroness G. de Rothschild

Göttingen was particularly adept. Hair pictures enjoyed great popularity for a time; they consisted of a sort of mosaic of different-coloured hairs. In Paris, Fontaine, Laine and Madame Moreau were especially famed for the delicacy of their work, and, at Coburg, Johann Andreas Scharf perfected himself in this laborious technique and trained a pupil, Walther, in it. Their pictures were mostly little scenes in the

No. 10. Isaac Oliver. *James I.*
Olim Howard Collection

languishing mode of the day; graves, urns, obelisks, as reminders of this transitory life; wreaths, weeping willows, and similar emblems of grief and mourning.

From the middle of the sixteenth century onwards a third style of miniature-painting was added to the other two—the enamel miniature. At his famous workshops at Limoges, where the art of covering metal articles with enamel was practised to perfection, Leonard Limousin began to paint portraits in enamel. The first portrait of this kind is said to be of Queen Eleanor, wife of Francis I., finished in 1536. This technique offers exceptional difficulties, because the artist can only command a limited number of colours, and these may alter considerably in the firing. For this reason the colour of the true Limoges enamel was not always suitable. Jean Toutin, a watch-maker of Châteaudun, perfected after 1632 the technique of

No. 11.   Isaac Oliver
Lady Arabella Stuart
Rijks Museum, Amsterdam

the Limoges enamel to such an extent, that he may almost be regarded as the inventor. Where Leonard Limousin was limited to six or seven colours, Toutin was master of so many tones that he could work in enamel as easily as if he were using water-colours. Henri Toutin, his son, trained Jean Petitot, generally regarded as the greatest artist who ever worked in this medium.

The miniature in enamel quickly won itself a privileged position, for to the beauty of the colours was added the advantage of their exceptional durability. Whereas miniatures in gouache or water-colours soon lost their freshness if they were exposed to the light, enamels kept their brightness without suffering. They were readily applied to snuff-boxes and

Bone. *Duchess of Portsmouth*

Hall. *The Artist*

watches. Voltaire had settled a colony of watch-makers at Ferney, and recommended them vigorously to his friends. In a letter dated 5th June, 1770, he praised them as the best craftsmen in Geneva: "they will decorate the cover with any portrait you wish in the most beautiful enamel."

Attempts were soon made to imitate the gloss and smoothness of the enamelled surface in some medium that was less laborious, and therefore less expensive. Lacquer answered the purpose; the painting was first carried out in water-colour and then lightly lacquered over with a coat of transparent varnish, which caused the colours to look brighter and gave a surface for the light to play on.

No. 12.   Isaac Oliver.   *Family Portrait*

In the beginning of the eighteenth century this art was practised by the craftsmen of Augsburg, it is said, but Robert Martin brought it to perfection a little later in Paris. He and his three brothers produced large and small pieces of furniture, which to-day fetch fantastic prices in the market if they bear the *"vernis Martin"* mark. Johann Heinrich Stobwasser made his name in Germany by his lacquer-work, which, after he started his first factory at Brunswick in 1764, found a tremendous sale, and was more or less successfully imitated. Jakob Bodemer, a native of Baden, who worked in Vienna about the end of the eighteenth century and beginning of the nineteenth, invented a peculiar method of combining lacquer with enamel.

Closely allied to enamel-painting is painting on porcelain, which possesses the same advantages and has the same

No. 13. Oliver. *The Digby Family*

difficulties to combat, for, in both cases, the colours change so much in the firing that even an experienced worker cannot always tell how they will come out.

Miniatures, no matter what the variations of technique, have one thing in common—their restricted size. Perhaps this was the reason for their neglect by critics, a neglect all the more deliberate, perhaps, in view of the eagerness shown by collectors and amateurs for their possession.

It seems almost impossible to resist their charm; around these little gems of art, so intimately connected with the ornaments or objects of daily use in past ages, there hangs an atmosphere of intimate tenderness quite absent from the productions of a more ambitious art. They still retain the first charm that breathed from them when they were pledges between living friends and lovers, when they were gazed upon by beauteous eyes and rested upon hearts that still beat knowing them for a link to bind ing them for a link to bind

No. 14.   Hoskins.
Elizabeth Stuart, sister of Charles I.
Rijks Museum, Amsterdam.

souls together across time and space. They seem to have rescued a moment's emotion from long-vanished days, and to hold it for us still; though we are strangers to the occasion which gave it birth, we cannot but feel wondrously stirred when enticing glances and smiling lips seem to tell us of beauty, love and friendship yet fresh and living, albeit we know they faded long ago. It is precisely this air of tenderness and sentiment that makes the miniature precious to many who are quite unaffected by a greater work of art and yet can feel love and sympathy for

No. 15.   Cooper.   *Oliver Cromwell*

the miniature without need of expert knowledge. This is undoubtedly one of the reasons which evoked the disparagement the miniature has met with in the history of art. Art critics have carried their aversion so far that they have even passed over in silence miniatures painted by recognised masters. The work of Hans Holbein has been endlessly sifted and checked, and yet there is uncertainty concerning his miniatures — a justifiable scepticism which tends, however, to cast more darkness than light on the matter. Many of the great masters started their career with miniature-work: Peter Lely, Raphael Mengs, Raeburn—to name a few; yet art critics have mostly dismissed this branch of their activities in a few words, as though the painters ought to be ashamed of their work.

This form of art came to depend more on delicacy and careful precision of workmanship than on the expression of artistic individuality, and no doubt this was the reason

No. 16.   Cooper.   *Lady Walter*

No. 17. Dixon. *Lady Chesterfield*

why these fruits of a minute industry were laid on one side, or shall we rather say allowed to languish forgotten, by the critics for whom style was the all-important touchstone of greatness. They even asserted, with a shrug of commiseration, that artists, such as Füger, who excelled in the field of miniature-work were cramping themselves by this peddling profession, and were held back from distinguishing themselves in the realm of high art. Carl von Lützow has expressed just such views with regard to Füger, whereas Ferdinand Laban, his latest biographer, remarks with justice that Füger's contributions to high art, his classical nullities, will never again be esteemed, and that it is the miniatures alone which make his name great.

Not until the evil fumes of pseudo-classicism were dissipated, and the art of the eighteenth century once more received the consideration it deserved, did pastels and miniatures venture to show themselves at exhibitions in the neighbourhood of easel pictures, and to awaken interest in themselves.

At first it was naturally in England, the land of great collectors, great collections and unbroken traditions, that repeated exhibitions made this precious material accessible

No. 18.   Zincke.   *Duchess of Buckingham*

to all, and attracted the notice of the historian. J. L. Propert was the first who endeavoured, in his *History of Miniature Art* (1887), to give an account of the English miniature in particular. He was followed by others, such as Dudley Heath and George C. Williamson; the latter has a goodly number of carefully written and excellently illustrated books to his credit, and has made this branch of art research his own domain. Williamson has also described Pierpont Morgan's miniature collection in a choice edition, whose lavish and sumptuous form could only be attempted by an American millionaire.

In France, the gifted Henri Bouchot has treated of the history of French miniatures.

No. 19.   Bartolozzi after Cosway.   *Maria Cosway*

Germany comes last, though not in the last place. After
the Vienna Congress Exhibition had brought to light treasures
of miniature-work in the possession of the Imperial family
and Austrian nobility, Franz Ritter wrote a brief sketch of
the history of miniature-portraits in Austria for the sumptuous
catalogue published by the Exhibition. Ferdinand Laban
laid the foundations of a worthy study of the work of Heinrich
Friedrich Füger, and recognised his importance as the greatest
of German miniature-painters. Finally, Ernst Lemberger
(*The Miniature Portrait in Germany*, 1550–1580) and Eduard
Leisching (*The Miniature Portrait in Austria*, 1750–1850)
have gathered together, classified and presented in excellent
fashion the gigantic mass of material which no one before
them had ventured to tackle. To-day picture-galleries no longer

disdain to exhibit the miniatures in their possession, as can
be seen, for instance, at the new Kaiser-Friedrich Museum
in Berlin. The biggest public collections of this kind are, of
course, to be found in those museums which make history and
the history of art and culture their chief interest, such as the
Hohenzollern Museum at Schloss Monbijou, the collections of
the Danish Royal house at Schloss Rosenborg and Schloss
Frederiksborg, which illustrate Danish history, a similar collection illustrating Swedish history at Schloss Grips-
holm, and many more.

No. 20.   Cosway.
Isabella, Marchioness of Hertford

Great portrait-painting
is a mirror of the times;
in an almost higher degree
is this true of the por-
trait-miniature, because it
is associated with a more
personal and individual
moment than the easel
picture or fresco. In the
manner of its treatment
and use the miniature is
more or less a handicraft,
and indeed associated with
such objects of personal
daily use that it seems to
retain something of the
nature of its original owner.

We can observe in a long series of miniatures not only
the development of the art itself, but also the way in which
society changes, taste alters, and needs increase in number
and refinement.

The painters of the sixteenth century aimed at truth and
sincerity, and tried with earnest conviction to represent each
man just as he was. The portraits of this period have something harsh and severe about them; even the most famous
beauties painted by these early artists appear to lack grace

No. 21. Cosway. *Lady Orde*

and charm, as though the painter really only had their features in his mind and never the soul which speaks from them. Utterly different were the seventeenth-century painters; they tried to fit their models to the fashion of beauty of the moment, and sacrificed likeness to an ideal. We realise this by the fact that it is very difficult to find, in the time of Louis XIV., the portrait of a society beauty in which one can tell what was really worn. Without exception the clothes were idealised, for even if the ladies' hair was dressed according to the fashion of the day, their attire was carried out in arbitrary style; for they all wanted to be represented as nymphs and goddesses, or at least famous beauties of antiquity. This flattery and falsification became a matter of course in the eighteenth century. Idealised as were the portraits of ladies of the court of the *roi soleil*, those of their daughters and granddaughters

No. 22.   Cosway.   *Anne, Duchess of Cumberland*
Olim Hodgkins Collection

had lost all truth and verisimilitude; powder, pencil and rouge prevented any serious characterisation, and gave only a lying mask of languishing sweetness and seductive loveliness. All society was subject to the same theory of art, and the more this developed and spread into all countries the more it became binding on them all.

The men and women of the sixteenth century have characteristic features, they are differentiated in their portraits; two hundred years later only the originals differed from one another—in their portraits these variations are of no account, for the painter was expected to subdue any difference to society's accepted ideal. The result of this could only be that portraits grew more and more similar. With the greater number of miniatures of the second half of the eighteenth century it is hard to distinguish one from another—the same glance, the same smile, the same rosy cheeks and red lips make it almost impossible to discover any characteristic features. In this respect the great masters—French or English —of this period are alike; they all pay homage to the same prejudices; but we must remember that they were bound to respect the aspirations of their fair clients, none of whom wished to appear less sweet and charming than her sweet and charming friend.

It is this state of affairs which makes it so difficult to attribute these miniatures to the right artists, and has resulted in the arbitrary designations that have been forced upon them by their owners.

No. 23. Cosway. *Lady Foster*

THE ENGLISH SCHOOL

ENGLAND stands in the front rank of those countries in which the art of miniature-painting has attained a high degree of excellence, for not only had she practised the art from very early days, but even in those early stages had seen it in its perfection.

English art is indebted to Hans Holbein for making popular this form of painting.

No. 24. Cosway. *Earl of Carlisle*

The great German painter studied miniature-work under Geraert Lucas Horembout, a Fleming who enjoyed great renown as a book illuminator, and has left some excellent specimens of his work; he it was who prepared part of the famous *Breviarum Grimani* at Venice. With but few intervals, Holbein dwelt in England from 1526 to his death in 1543, and enjoyed high favour at the court of Henry VIII. He has immortalised the king, the various queens and the court in oils, drawings and miniatures. He carried out the last-mentioned in water-colour on paper and used for preference the backs of playing-cards, as we have already mentioned. If everything which is ascribed to him in English and foreign collections were really by him, the master must have been of positively amazing fertility.

22

Moreover, it is in precisely this part of Holbein's work, as Paul Ganz,' his latest biographer, admits, that originals and copies are so hard to differentiate; all the more as not even a catalogue of all the miniatures ascribed to him as yet exists. After severe sifting, about ten examples, all in tempera on paper, survive criticism. The wonderful head of the Man with a Lily (Plate I.), which bears the date 1533, was long held to be a self-portrait—wrongly so when we compare it with the authentic portraits of himself. The one in the Wallace Collection (p. 2) is regarded to-day as having un-questionably the best claim to authenticity. Next to it comes the one in the possession of the Duke

No. 25. Cosway.
Countess of Salisbury

of Buccleuch at Montagu House, from Horace Walpole's famous collection at Strawberry Hill. Whatever miniatures of Henry VIII. and his wives are to be met with in English hands are assumed to be by Holbein, and Horace Walpole assures us that many more works of this kind were lost in the burning of White-hall in about 1698. If the por-traits of the king and his fourth wife (p. 4) are by Holbein, they must have been painted in the early months of 1540. After the death of Jane Seymour the king wished, for political reasons,

No. 26. Cosway. *Lady Harcourt*

to wed a princess of a German Protestant house, and his choice fell on Anne, a daughter of Duke John III. of Jülich-Cleve-

Berg. Holbein is said to have contributed not a little to the king's decision by his very flattering portrait of the lady, then twenty-five years old. The wedding took place on the 6th January, 1540, and in July of the same year the royal Blue-beard was once more free to marry his fifth wife, the Lady Katherine Howard, whom he beheaded two years later. Henry did not make the painter suffer for his deceptive picture, but Thomas Cromwell, his chancellor, who had persuaded the

No. 27.   Cosway.
Anne, Marchioness of Townshend
Olim Hodgkins Collection

king to this match and had been strongly against the divorce, atoned on the scaffold for the crime, amongst others, of pro-curing his master a wife devoid of charm. The despised lady lived till 1557 in a remote English castle, and died only one year before her step-daughter, Queen Mary.

A portrait of a Young Lady of twenty-three years of age, carried out in water-colours on the back of a playing-card, represents a member of the Pem-berton family, whose arms are on the outside of the medal-lion. The lady was formerly thought to be the Duchess of Norfolk, and it was under that name that this beautiful portrait was sold by auction at Christie's in 1904, and bought by Messrs. Duveen for £2750, probably for Pierpont Morgan's collection.

Nicholas Hilliard (1547–1619) and Isaac Oliver (1556–1617) are not so much pupils as imitators of Holbein, and modelled themselves closely on him with regard to their technique. Hilliard held at the courts of Elizabeth and James I. the same position as Holbein at that of Henry VIII.; all miniature-portraits of the Virgin Queen are ascribed to him. He is more interesting for his rendering of the rich costume of

Hall.   *Princess Louise of Prussia*

Augustin.   *Young Woman at the Piano*

No. 28.   Cosway.   *Thomas Townley, Esq.*
Olim Hodgkins Collection

the period than for his characterisation of the faces, which often
appear weak and insipid. He has painted the queen (p. 7), in
the fantastic toilet which that great lady delighted in. Elizabeth, virtuous perforce by reason of some physical disability,
was inordinately vain and coquettish. Amongst her belongings
at her death were found eighty wigs and six thousand dresses,
a supply which, owing to the costliness of the materials,
represents a considerable amount of capital. The older she
grew, the more her love of adornment increased, and travellers
who beheld her during the last twenty years of the sixteenth
century cannot say enough about the "incredible magnificence" of her attire. In this portrait, which must have been
made in 1558, soon after her accession, she still has youth
and charm.

Lady Jane Grey (p. 6), likewise bedizened according to
the fashion and wearing the red and white Tudor roses in

c

her hair, is the unhappy woman who was Queen of England for a week. She was a great-granddaughter of Henry VII.

No. 29. Cosway. *Maria, Countess of Lindsey*. Family Collection   No. 30. Cosway. *Charlotte, Countess of Lindsey*. Family Collection

and wife to Guildford Dudley, son of the Duke of Northumberland, and she was said to have been named as his successor by Edward VI. on his deathbed. She was crowned on the

No. 31. Cosway. *Portrait of a Young Man*

6th July, 1553, but taken prisoner by her rival, Mary Tudor, on the 12th July, and beheaded at the Tower of London.

The portrait of Mary Tudor (p. 9) shows the unhappy daughter of Henry VIII. and Catherine of Arragon—a woman whose unpleasing personality and appearance deprives her of the sympathy that is her due. The queen, whom nobody loved, forms a striking contrast to that other Mary whose many friends were in the end the cause of her downfall.

No. 32.   Cosway.   *Henry Banks, Esq.*
Olim Hodgkins Collection

Elizabeth had no security while her too popular rival was alive, and so the story ends at Fotheringhay on 18th February, 1587.

Though it is possible or probable that Hilliard painted Mary Stuart from life, it is certain, according to the researches of Williamson, that the portrait of Gabrielle d'Estrées was founded on an engraving by Thomas de Leu. When Henry IV. met the lady of his heart at her father's castle during the French Civil War, she was barely twenty years of age, and inspired the king with such a passion that he did not

No. 33.   Cosway.   *The Princess Lubomirski*
Miss White's Collection

hesitate to put his life in danger merely to behold her. She was made Duchesse de Beaufort and lived at court not only beautiful, but gifted and so marvellously lovable that, according to Agrippa d'Aubigné, she had scarcely an enemy. To these few, however, belonged a very powerful one, the Duc de Sully, and to him her early death is said to be due. In spite of opposition from every side, Henry had decided to marry Gabrielle and make her his queen, when suddenly, a few days before the marriage, on 10th April, 1599, a horrible death overtook her. Immediately after eating an orange she was seized with terrible convulsions, and her body and face were so horribly distorted and disfigured that no one could look at the corpse without a shudder. Blin de Sainmore,

Poinsinet and Sauvigny have, in epic and tragedy, celebrated the famous Gabrielle and her fate.

Isaac Oliver was a pupil of Hilliard, and the Italian Federigo Zucchero, who lived in England from 1574 and earned his bread by miniature - painting. Whether the portrait of Mary Stuart which is usually ascribed to him has greater claims to authenticity than that by Hilliard is uncertain; at any rate it is more attractive, and permits us some belief in the beauty of that unhappy queen. Sir Richard Holmes, however, believed it to represent the Countess of Nottingham, a lady

No. 34. Shelley. *Mother and Child*
Olim Marshall Hall Collection

of Queen Elizabeth's Court, whose notoriety was due to her responsibility for the execution of the Earl of Essex. Elizabeth had, when he was high in her favour, given him a ring, and promised to grant him a request if he would send this ring back to her and remind her of her promise. When he was sentenced, she waited anxiously for this message from her former favourite, and as it never came she allowed the law to take its course. Elizabeth heard with despair from the countess on her deathbed that Essex had given her the ring to send to the queen, and she had withheld it out of jealousy.

The Family Portrait (p. 11) shows Oliver on a level with

his English master. The jewellery and large lace collars are reproduced with minute exactitude down to the smallest details of the pattern, whilst the features and expression of the faces are perhaps a trifle insipid. His portrait of Lady Arabella Stuart (p. 10) now in the Rijks Museum represents the

No. 35.   Cosway.   *Hugh Seymour as a boy*
Family Collection

daughter of the Earl of Lennox. Neither Queen Elizabeth nor James I. was at all well-disposed towards her, and she more than once had the opportunity to reflect on their idiosyncrasies in the Tower. In 1610 she married William Seymour, and seems to have been sufficiently in favour at court to contemplate attending the marriage of the Elector Frederick with the Princess Elizabeth, for which she ordered a dress costing £1500. She never wore it, however, for the king sent her for the last time to the gloomy fortress on the Thames, where she died in 1615.

Isaac's son and pupil, Peter Oliver (1601–47), carries on the tradition to the time of Van Dyck, the portrait-painter of the court and the English nobility. The charm and grace which the great Fleming imparted to his portraits of lords and ladies, that air of careless elegance which hangs about everything he painted, brought both society and artists

No. 36. Peter Oliver. *Lord Willoughby*
Olim Willoughby Collection

themselves under his spell. Everyone wanted to be painted by Van Dyck, and every painter wanted to paint like him. The cult of beauty which Van Dyck carried on to the detriment of characterisation was followed by Gottfried Kneller and Peter Lely, and the miniature-painters also succumbed to this influence. Peter Oliver keeps to the Van Dyck manner, and Walpole considered his portrait of Lady Lucy Percy the most perfect miniature in the world and gave £100 for it— an enormous sum for the eighteenth century. Oliver often copied directly from Van Dyck; the Digby Family (p. 12) is an exact copy of the great painting in the possession of the Duke of Portland at Welbeck Abbey. He has also repeated Van Dyck's portrait of Lady Venetia Digby on her death-bed; she died in 1633, barely thirty years old.

John Hoskins (*d.* 1664) also follows in the wake of Van Dyck, and his portrait of Queen Henrietta Maria was copied from a painting by him. The wife of Charles I. and youngest daughter of Henry IV. is represented in the height of her

No. 37. Shelley. *Unknown Lady*

power. After her son had been restored to the throne lost by his father through his own fault, she lived at Somerset House, but often journeyed back to Paris, where she died in 1669, and was buried in the royal vault at St. Denis. Van Dyck and Hoskins have flattered her. When the queen paid a visit to her niece Sophia of the Palatinate (later Electress of Hanover), the latter, misled by portraits she had seen, expected to find in her aunt a most beautiful woman, and was grievously disappointed to find her bent, with long thin arms and prominent teeth. John Hoskins has also painted himself wearing, according to the fashion, a shirt richly ornamented with insertions and edgings of lace.

Samuel Cooper (*d.* 1672), the nephew and pupil of Hoskins, was the painter of the

No. 38. John Smart. *M.A.R.* 1787
Olim Wertheimer Collection

Commonwealth and of that Puritan society which presented such a striking contrast in appearance, speech and behaviour to the society of Charles I.'s court. Samuel Cooper is considered by Englishmen to be one of their greatest artists, and he is, without doubt, the first English miniaturist with a quite individual style; though he developed under the influence of Van Dyck, his works have a power and energy that is often lacking in the creations of his master. He turned his attention to painting on card in gouache, which he handled in a broad and free manner. Cooper has left us portraits of Cromwell, Milton and other great men of the time which breathe forth the harsh and earnest spirit of the day. The portrait of the Protector (p. 14) has always aroused the liveliest admiration. Cromwell himself is said to have remarked that the painter had surpassed himself, and Horace Walpole used to say that if most of Cooper's miniatures were enlarged they would equal Van Dyck's paintings, but that his Cromwell would throw Van Dyck into the shade. In the portrait of Lady Walter (p. 14) we see, perhaps, Lucy Waters, mistress of Charles II. and mother of the Duke of Monmouth.

Samuel's brother, Alexander Cooper, was also an excellent miniature-painter. He worked almost exclusively abroad. In 1632 he painted, at the Hague, the whole of the Winter King's family; twelve small portraits in one medallion. In the next decade he went north and worked at the court of Queen Christina and King Charles Gustavus X., and in the sixteen-fifties he was at Copenhagen, where he did likenesses of all the members of the royal house.

With the Coopers a dazzling period of English miniature art came to an end, for they had no immediate successors. Laurence Crosse (d. 1742) and Bernard Lens (d. 1725) excelled not so much in portrait-painting as in reproducing small versions of pictures by Rubens or Van Dyck. The only artist who enjoyed any fame or esteem at this time was Nathaniel Dixon. Nothing is known of his life; he painted Elizabeth Savile, Lady Chesterfield (p. 15), wife of Philip Stanhope, third Earl of Chesterfield. She became the mother in 1694 of

Philip Dormer Stanhope, the Lord Chesterfield of the famous *Letters to his Son*—those letters full of educative zeal and worldly wisdom which nevertheless failed to prevent that son from growing up a fool, heedless of all the witty advice his father had lavished on him.

Christian Friedrich Zincke (1683–1767), born in Germany, worked in England beside Dixon. If the portrait of the Duchess of Buckingham and her son (p. 16) is indeed by him, it is hard to understand the popularity he enjoyed and which was in fact very great, for the artist was so overwhelmed with commissions, that he had to raise his price from twenty to thirty guineas a portrait because he could not do justice to so many orders.

No. 39.   *Medallion, with eye and lock of hair of Gerhard von Kügelgen*

In the second half of the seventeenth century miniatures on enamel became very popular in England; Petitot had first made them known while on a brief visit, but it was really Charles Boit who introduced the art into England. Born in Sweden in 1663, of French parents, he came to London in 1683, and laboured for a long time as a jeweller and enamel-worker. His enamel-work found such favour that he received as much as £500 for single portraits, a huge sum for the period.

English miniature art, after a long period of stagnation and even retrogression, enters into a new phase of brilliance with Richard Cosway. He was born in 1740, and exhibited in 1760 for the first time; after 1761 he devoted himself exclusively to miniature-work. His portrait of Mrs. Fitzherbert, the beloved and, in secret, the wife of the Prince of Wales, brought him into touch with the Court and drew the attention of Society upon him. He soon became the popular craze, for he understood better than any of his predecessors or contemporaries the flattering art of a painter of Beauty. He paid too much homage in this direction, it is true, and made a fetish of beauty, as Dudley Heath truly says. He set up a seductive ideal; languishing or melancholy eyes in a delicate fresh-tinted face crowned by a wealth of hair too great to grow naturally on any head. Here was the novel-reader's ideal; the Lovelace or Clarissa Harlowe, with whose fate men and women of sensibility so deeply sympathised and with whom they

No. 40. *Eyes of Queen Louise and her four eldest Children*

longed to compare themselves. This sentimental quality in Cosway is all the more bewitching because the painter had absolute command over the technical side of his art, and each one of his portraits was a little gem of exquisite taste. He himself was only happy in the great world, and his chosen element was Society. He lived in splendid style in the former Schomberg Palace in Pall Mall, and when, later, he moved to Oxford Street, his new home was a marvel of comfort and elegance. He gave brilliant receptions and parties, and was visited by the best society; for though he himself was vain and a dandy and a constant butt for good and bad witticisms, he possessed in his wife Maria a magnet which kept his house always full. Maria Hadfield (p. 17) came to England as a very young girl with Angelica Kauffmann, and married Cosway, then already famous. She loved dress and luxury as much as he did, but when she was fantastically dressed, she had the advantage over her ugly husband of great beauty.

No. 41. John Smart. *Unknown Lady*. 1802
Collection Monsieur Stettiner

She was, moreover, both lovable, witty and musical, and painted in miniature at least as well as did her husband. The glory of the Cosways lasted for many years. Shadows began to threaten when the painter was so little able to dissemble his sympathy with the French Revolution that the Prince Regent withdrew his favour. His wife fell ill, their only child died, Cosway's right hand was injured by a paralytic stroke, and their circumstances grew very straitened, for the great expenses of their extravagantly run ménage had swallowed up the large sums they had received. Their house and its contents was sold, and the artist on whom fortune had smiled so long, died just as he was setting up a small and modest home in the Edgware Road. After his death Maria Cosway returned to her home in Italy, where she founded a "College for Young Ladies" at Lodi, and devoted herself to the education of young English girls. She died in the eighteen-thirties, and a few years before was given the rank of baroness by her sovereign, the Emperor Francis I. of Austria.

If Cosway suffers from too great a uniformity of sweet-

Augustin. *Citizeness Fanny Charrin*

Augustin.   *Mlle. Bianchi*

ness, that can be explained by reason of the great speed with which he must have worked. He is said to have had twelve or fourteen people sit to him in one day, so that he had to work at a rate which, if maintained, must adversely affect the quality of his work.

His portrait of George III. (Plate II.), the monarch to whose obstinate wrong-headedness England owed the loss of America, belongs to his best work. The painter has not suppressed an expression of anxiety that betrays an abnormal sensitiveness. George III. ascended the throne at the age of twenty-two, so ignorant that he spoke neither English nor German correctly, had repeated attacks of melancholia, and finally became incurably insane and died in 1820 blind and without recovering his reason.

No. 42.   John Smart.
Unknown Lady

The portrait of the Marchioness of Hertford (p. 18) represents Isabella Anna Ingram Shepherd, who married Francis Seymour, Marquis of Hertford, and became the mother, in 1800, of the famous art collector of that name. Thackeray has depicted him, not very sympathetically, in *Vanity Fair*. The Wallace Collection originated with him. Lady Orde (p. 19) was Margaret Stephens, who wedded John Orde, the first baronet of that name, in 1790, and died the same year. Cosway gives her the same half-fantastic vestal virgin attire in which a princess of Courland was painted at the same period by Angelica Kauffmann. Mrs. Stuart Wortley Mackenzie was Margaret, daughter of Sir David Cunningham, Bart., and mother of the first Lord Wharncliffe. Lady Harcourt (p. 23) was the wife of the third Lord Harcourt; the Countess of Salisbury (p. 23), Maria Amelia, was a daughter of Wills, first Marquis of Downshire, and married James, first Marquis of Salisbury. This unfortunate lady perished in a fire at Hatfield House on the 27th November, 1835.

Cosway also painted William Spencer Cavendish, later sixth Duke of Devonshire, when a boy. He was born in 1790 and died a bachelor in 1858, in spite of the snares

No. 43.   Smart.   *Lord Rivers*

of mothers with marriageable daughters. Countess Boigne, who met him in London in 1818, relates in what a mischievous spirit he baffled those same eager daughters. He had just returned from the Continent and spoke with delight of the new waltz and with what grace and elegance French women danced it. At that time the waltz was barred in good society, just as the tango was a hundred years later. But what will not a maiden do for a good match, and a duke at that! At the next ball all the young girls were dancing the waltz with as much abandon as possible, when the duke, after looking on for some time, declared he could never marry a young girl capable of dancing such an immodest dance.

The portrait of Lady Foster (p. 21) represents the duke's step - mother. When a girl, Lady Elizabeth Hervey, daughter of the Earl of Bristol, she married John Thomas Foster. She entered the household of the Duke of Devonshire as governess to his natural daughter by Miss Spencer. She quickly became the intimate friend of the Duchess Georgiana, and, after her husband's death, went travelling with her on the Continent. She could have married

No. 44.   Smart.   *Portrait*

Gibbon, the famous historian, had she wished, but she preferred to live in a three-cornered relationship that proved satisfactory to all, with her friend and her friend's husband.

After the death of her friend Georgiana in 1806, she married the duke by whom she had so long been beloved and who died in 1814. Countess Lulu Thürheim, a lady whom one cannot accuse of speaking with undue mildness or indulgence of her contemporaries,

No. 45.   Unknown.   *Snuff-box of second half of the Eighteenth Century*

says concerning the members of English Society in Rome, "Their faults are easily seen, their virtues are hidden by the modesty of their owners." She bears enthusiastic witness to the qualities of the Duchess of Devonshire when she writes:

Her death (1824) is an irreparable loss for Rome. She patronised Art and antiquarian research with prudence and generosity. Her house was the meeting-place for artists and foreigners; writers lauded its magnificence, the poor blessed her for her help. All her life she followed the inspiration of her fiery spirit which led her into many errors, but was bound up with so much gentleness of character and sympathy with the weaknesses and afflictions of her fellow-men, that no one ever presumed to judge her harshly.

No. 46. Plimer. *Lady Ravensworth, Lady Paul and Miss Simpson.   Olim* Wertheimer Collection

George Howard, Earl of Carlisle and Viscount Morpeth (p. 22) (*b.* 1773, *d.* 1848), married Georgiana Dorothea Caven-

No. 47.   Plimer.   *Miss Caroline Calvert*
Olim Verney Collection

dish, daughter of the fifth Duke of Devonshire. Lady Paget, another Cosway subject, was Augusta Jane Fane (*b.* 1786), daughter of the Earl of Westmoreland, and married in 1804 John Parker, first Earl Morley who divorced her on the 14th February, 1809; she married Arthur Paget the same day. Until the death of Queen Charlotte, who married George III. in 1761 and died in 1818, ladies with an interesting past had an uncomfortable position in Society, for the queen never received a divorced woman, and the fact that they could not be received at Court was a heavy burden.

Cosway repeatedly painted the two Bertie sisters. They were the daughters of Peregrine, third Duke of Ancaster. Lady Priscilla married the first Lord Gwydyr and became, through the death of her brother Robert, Baroness Willoughby de Eresby in her own right. Her sister, Lady Georgiana, became Marchioness of Cholmondeley.

An extraordinary number of Cosway's portraits represent unknown persons. For lack of information we must reckon Lady Elizabeth Aldeburgh among them. They are the harder to indentify because their invariable prettiness has reduced them all to an unfortunate similarity. There are many Cosway forgeries, but as he only signed his works on the back, miniatures which have his name in front should be regarded with mistrust.

Cosway's style was too "pretty" not to be imitated by all his contemporaries. All tried to reproduce that grace and charm of bearing, softness of shape, able and delicate gradation of tone as completely as did the celebrated and fashionable artist, and this often makes impossible any trustworthy attribution of the unsigned miniatures.

W. H. Craft was originally a painter on porcelain at the Bow factory. He has done an excellent enamel-portrait of Sir Joshua Reynolds which is now at the Ashmolean at Oxford. The portrait was not taken from life, but probably from the self-portrait of the great artist which he made in

No. 48. Plimer. *Miss Gunning* (*later Duchess of Argyll*)

1786 and left to the Academy. He was the first president of that institution, which was founded in 1768, and a painter who enjoyed fame and glory during his lifetime to an extent granted to few before or after him. A great artist and a handsome, well-bred man, title, honour and wealth positively showered upon him. He painted everyone of importance or position in England during his life (1723–1792), and exercised an influence which extended far beyond the bounds of England, thanks to the hundreds of engravings made from his pictures.

Not only does his name connote a definite phase of English art, it has also become typical of the style and fashion of the time. If he has a fault, it is the poor lasting quality of his pictures. He was fond of experimenting with ground-colours, of mixing

D

colours, etc., and with such unfortunate results that his pictures began to darken after a short time, and to look insignificant. The

No. 49. Plimer. *Young Woman*

purchasers were naturally far from satisfied, and one of them made the suggestion that he should pay for his painting by instalments, which he would keep up only as long as the picture lasted!

Samuel Shelley, a contemporary and imitator of Cosway, excelled in miniatures of mothers and children—a fashion favoured by the mode of the moment (p. 32). This combination is not very general, however, and portraits like that of the Duchess of Buckingham and her son (p. 16) are rarities and quite different in manner from those of later date. Here, two persons are posed near one another in rather clumsy juxta-

position, whereas in the second half of the century, mothers with their children are depicted with over-flowing family feeling—a harmonious group. Family affection was the fashion, after Rousseau's attempt to drive the over-cultured Society of his day back to Nature, and the English novel, through Richardson in particular, supported this taste. It suddenly became good form for mothers to nurse their children, and they might be seen to rise from the dinner-table to carry out their duties and silence the

No. 50. Plimer.
Mrs. T. Somers Cocks

little screamer *coram publico*! The earliest picture in this tender genre is probably Bernard Lens's Lady Harley and her daughter painted in 1717; at the end of the century Cosway, Plimer, Shelley and others made numerous portraits of this kind.

George Engleheart rivalled Cosway in the representation of beautiful ladies decked out in mighty perruques and still mightier hats. The portrait of George IV. (Plate III.) shows him in his early youth when, as Prince of Wales, he was still languishing at the feet of Mrs. Fitzherbert, to whom he was secretly married in 1785. His contemporaries called him the First Gentleman of Europe, but posterity has nothing good to say of him. His dissolute life and scandalous behaviour to his unhappy wife, Caroline of Brunswick, have left stains on his reputation which can never be removed. In 1811, at the age of forty-nine, he became regent for his insane father, and from 1820–1830 reigned as George IV.

No. 51. Cosway? *William IV.*

Engleheart invented a new affectation that immediately became the fashion. He painted Mrs. Fitzherbert's eye for the Prince of Wales—a conceit that was far too pretty not to be at once imitated. Paintings of eyes on bracelets and medallions became all the rage, and many years later the painter Caroline Bardua maintained herself by this means in the hard times which followed in Germany after the Wars of Liberation. From 1811 she frequently painted the eye of Princess Christine of Schwarzburg-Sondershausen, who was very proud of this beautiful feature of hers. Gerhard von Kügelgen also began his artistic career with eye-painting. Prince Tschertorinsky in St. Petersburg paid him in 1798 one hundred roubles for a miniature of this kind. His family still possess a painting of his own eye and lock of hair in a medallion (p. 34). One of the keepsakes of Queen Louise found amongst her things is a small painting of the eyes of herself and her children (p. 35). Sir William Ross and Anthony Stewart were later followers of this fashion. In England it was quite recently practised. There are medallions in the collection of the Grand Duke of Hesse containing paintings of the eyes of most of the members of Queen Victoria's family. Even in 1915 W. Horst executed a commission of this kind. No matter how lovingly the painter devotes himself to the work, however, we are convinced there is but little expression in these pictures; the mouth is a far more charac-

No. 52.   Bone.   *Duchess of Devonshire*

teristic feature than the eye. When it was a fashionable Society game to try and recognise people by their eyes alone, how many amusing mistakes were made!

John Smart belongs to Cosway's circle and painted a portrait of the charming Mrs. Cosway in 1784. This beautiful woman was frequently painted—usually in slightly fantastic garb—and even more eagerly immortalised by the engravers of the day.

Lord Rivers (p. 38) is Horace Beckford, third Lord Rivers.

Andrew Plimer (*b.* 1764) and his brother Nathaniel were pupils of Cosway, and both popular miniaturists in their day.

Augustin. *Mlle. Duchesnois*

Isabey. *Mlle. Lange*

Andrew's most important work is the portrait of the three Rushout sisters, commonly called, like the beautiful sisters themselves, the Three Graces. They were the daughters of John Rushout, who was made first Lord Northwick in 1797. The Hon. Harriet Rushout married Sir Charles Cockerell in 1808 and died in 1851; the Hon. Anne Rushout remained a spinster, her betrothed having died suddenly three days before the wedding. She died in 1849. The third sister, Elizabeth, was considered the most beautiful. She married twice; first Mr. Sydney Bowles, and later Mr. John Wallis Greave. Plimer has also

No. 53. Unknown. *English Officer*

done a portrait of their relative, the Lady Caroline Rushout. He exhibited this miniature at the Royal Academy in 1803, and was much praised for it. The Duchess of Argyll (p. 41) is one of the three famous Gunning sisters. They were the daughters of quite a poor country squire, and when they came up to London for the season they turned the heads of every man in Society and made brilliant marriages. Elizabeth married the Duke of Hamilton and, *en secondes noces*, the fifth Duke of Argyll. She died in 1790.

Mrs. Thomas Somers Cocks (p. 42) is a *belle inconnue* and has left us no other remembrance of her life than her pretty face.

No. 54. Mansion. *Unknown Lady*

The delightful portrait of the Duke of Clarence (p. 43) is probably by Cosway or one of his pupils. A son of George III. and born in 1765, he became the hero of Caroline von Linsingen's romantic love-story. She was secretly married to the

English prince in 1790 at Pyrmont, but he soon left his young and wildly-infatuated wife and returned to England. She fell into a serious illness that ended apparently in her death. She was to have been buried had not a young doctor Meinecke prevented this and saved her. She awakened from the trance into which she had fallen, and married her rescuer, with whom she lived for many years. The Duke of Clarence consoled himself in the arms of Mrs. Jordan, by whom he had ten children. In 1818 he married Princess Adelaide of Sachsen-Meiningen, and succeeded his brother, George IV., in 1830 as William IV. Greville in his *Journal* writes thus of him:

> Hitherto his life had been passed in gloom and neglect, in lamentable poverty, surrounded by a swarm of bastards. He had no friends and no one esteemed him, so ludicrous was he in his manners and childish curiosity. He was invited nowhere, and no one offered him any civilities. Canning nominated him Lord High Admiral. In this position he distinguished himself only by the absurd speeches he made and an unusual turbulence and wildness of demeanour which pointed to a coming mental derangement.

He was followed by Queen Victoria in 1837.

Henry Bone, a contemporary of Cosway's, was born at Truro in 1755, and died in London in 1834. He was Court painter to George III. and George IV., and was famous for his enamels. He was fond of copying old portraits, and that of the Duchess of Portsmouth (Plate IV.) is one of his best. Louise Renée de Kéroualle was born in Brittany and came to the Court of Charles II. in the suite of the Duchess Henrietta of Orleans, his sister. She became lady-in-waiting to the queen, Catherine of Braganza, and the king's mistress. He made her Duchess of Portsmouth in 1673, and her son was Charles Lennox, Duke of Richmond. She was the most hated of all the king's numerous mistresses, and it was thought to be owing to her influence that English politics were dragged at the heels of France. She was also incredibly extravagant and squandered money right and left. When Charles II. was dying she took care to have him received into the Catholic Church. After his death she returned to Paris, where she died in 1734. A series of

Bone's enamels similar to this one — eighty-five copies of portraits of famous men and women of Queen Elizabeth's Court—was put up for auction in London in 1856 and fetched £5000. Bone excelled in miniatures also. The Duchess of Devonshire (p. 44) represents Georgiana, daughter of Earl Spencer, who was born in 1757 and married to the duke in 1774. She was the intimate friend of Lady Elizabeth Foster, her husband's mistress and second wife, and consoled herself for her husband's unfaithfulness in the arms of Lord Grey. She is said to have been one of the most charming women of her day, and was for many years the leader of London Society. She died in 1806.

In the nineteenth century three Scotchmen continued the great tradition of English miniature-painting. They were: Andrew Robertson, Ross and Thorburn. Robertson was born at Aberdeen in 1777 and came to London in 1801 to perfect himself at the Royal Academy. He was soon able to raise the price of his miniatures from £4 or £5 to £11, and died in 1845, a much appreciated artist. Thorburn lived to see the rise and spread of photography, which discouraged all artistic activities, if, as in the case of lithography, it did not completely throttle them.

No. 55. Clouet.
Catherine de Médicis

No. 56. Clouet.
King Charles IX. of France

THE FRENCH SCHOOL

THE history of French miniature-painting begins, as has been mentioned above, with Jean Clouet, whose position at Court was inherited by his son, François Clouet, called Janet. He was the painter of the last Valois, and made portraits of all those whom Catherine de Médicis, her husband and sons gathered round them. A head of Francis I. at the Louvre and another portrait of this king on horseback, which is in the Uffizi at Florence, are the best examples of the elder Clouet, whose works were not very numerous. His son has left a great number of large paintings, miniatures and drawings which, on account of their powerful technique, have often been ascribed to Holbein.

The portraits of the Queen-Mother, Catherine de Médicis (p. 47), and her son Charles IX. (p.. 47), are in a gold and enamel medallion in the collection of the Imperial family at Vienna. Clouet must have painted them in 1570 when Charles IX. became affianced to the Archduchess Elizabeth, daughter of the Emperor Maximilian II. At the same time Benvenuto Cellini's famous salt-cellar came with other gifts from the French Court to the Hofburg at Vienna. Catherine de Médicis (1519–1589) played such an infamous rôle in history that she became a favourite subject for the poet when the historical romance and the historical play came into its own. Charles IX. (1550–1574) enjoys the sorry fame of having at best raised no protest at the massacre on St. Bartholomew's Eve. He died of consumption, and his widow, being childless, returned to Austria, where she died in 1592 in a convent at Vienna.

No. 57. Petitot. *Portrait of a Lady*
Collection Mme. Orban

There is so little to relate of French miniatures of the rest
of the sixteenth century and, indeed, of the greater part of
the seventeenth, that French authors, writing of this branch
of art, pass over this period in silence, and prefer to begin
with the middle of the eighteenth century; Henry Bouchot is
one of these.

There would, indeed, be no artist of importance to mention
in this period did not Jean Petitot, a French-Swiss, fill the
gap. He was born in Geneva in 1607, and learnt the art of
enamel-work, first in Paris and then, in the sixteen-thirties,
in London. He schooled himself in the works of Van Dyck,
whom he frequently copied, and enjoyed great favour at the
Court of Charles I. On the fall of the Monarchy he went to
Paris, where he received the same privileges at the French
Court as he had at the English. He copied, in enamel, the
works of the greatest portrait-painters of the day—Mignard,
Philippe de Champaigne, Nanteuil, etc. His chef-d'œuvre is
a miniature of Cardinal Mazarin, his most famous production
a golden box, once in the possession of Alfred de Rothschild,
showing fourteen portraits of the most famous beauties of
the Court at Versailles. Being a Protestant he was imprisoned
on the revocation of the Edict of Nantes, and was lucky
enough to escape to Switzerland, where he died well on in

No. 58. Boucher. *Venus and Cupid*

years at Vevey in 1691. His son Jean Louis was almost as much admired for his enamels as his father, to whom, however, he is in certain slight respects inferior.

Miniatures in enamel were much appreciated at the Court of the *roi soleil*, and a Swede, Friedrich Bruckmann, distinguished himself in this art, his enamels fetching sixty francs each in the last years of the century.

The great French portrait-painters of this epoch, Largillière (1656–1746), Massé (1687–1767), etc., made small portraits, but cannot precisely claim to be miniaturists. A miniature ascribed to Largillière in Pierpont Morgan's collection represents Nicolas Boileau, the famous author of the mock-epic *Le Lutrin*; he lived from 1636–1711. Boileau was of a frank and honourable nature, and on one occasion when Louis XIV. was complaining of the low level of the repertoire at the French theatre, he replied in Madame de

No. 59. Boucher. *Mythological Scene*

Maintenon's presence that it was due to the miserable plays of Scarron, of which the public were so fond. As Scarron was the first husband of the marquise, who had for some time been secretly married to the king, this was a distinctly candid reply.

Rosalba Carriera, famous as pastellist, painted some miniatures on her visit to Paris; one of Louis XIV. as a child, one of the great financier, John Law, at the height of his power,

No. 60.   Cazaubon after Nattier.
Louise Henriette de Bourbon-Conti

and his little daughter who, with her dowry of seventeen millions, was the richest heiress in France. A short time afterwards her father's millions melted into air.

François Boucher (1703–1770), the great man of Louis XV.'s reign, found an artistic formula for the sensuous *joie de vivre* of Rococo, and expressed the taste of the age in frescoes and wall decorations. His voluptuous and amorous nymphs and goddesses (p. 50), love-sick Arcadians, and similar mythological ambiguities, won themselves a great place in the world of art. It is doubtful whether he himself painted any miniatures, and we are inclined to credit Baudouin and smaller men with the execution of most of those ascribed to him.

The French miniaturists of this time were hampered by routine; Cazaubon's portrait of the Duchess of Orleans (p. 51) is an example of their art. This is a painting from Nattier, and the Duchesse Louise Henriette de Bourbon-Conti is represented as Hebe. She was born in 1726, married in 1743, and died in 1759. The artist was much occupied in the service of the Court with its *menus-plaisirs*; he painted Louis XV., Marie Lesczynska and the royal princesses, receiving three hundred livres for each miniature.

No. 61.   Baudouin (after Boucher).   *Love's Message*

The Drouais, father and son, are amongst the best French miniaturists; Hubert (1699–1767), the father, made numerous portraits of the Marquise de Pompadour, and François Hubert (1727–1775), the son, had a great vogue. He aimed at new style and treatment. His Family Portrait of the Beauharnais (p. 53) is an example of his striving after originality. The boy is Vicomte Alexandre de Beauharnais, who was guillotined in 1794 when a general of the French Republic, and only thirty-four years old. He was the first husband of Joséphine Tascher de la Pagerie (who later became Napoleon's Empress), and father of Eugène de Beauharnais and Queen Hortense. His mother's portrait hangs round his neck and he holds a likeness of his father, the Marquis de Beauharnais, who was many years Governor of Martinique. In technique and colour this is one of Drouais' best miniatures.

Two foreigners helped to put fresh impulse into the stagnant life of French miniature art, and caused it to rise to great heights. One was Jean Etienne Liotard (1702–1789), a native of Geneva, who as artist and business man came to seek

No. 62.   Drouais.   *The Beauharnais Family*

congenial society abroad. He had travelled in many lands, including Turkey, and when he returned to Western Europe, understood well how to attract the public. In the Rococo period, when even men powdered and rouged, he elected to grow a long beard, and when he had attracted a great deal of notice by this amazing boldness, he increased the peculiarity of his appearance by putting on Oriental dress and affecting brusque manners towards the spoilt children of Paris Court circles.

At Vienna he was greatly favoured by Maria Theresa, who made him royal gifts. In Paris he created a furore on his first appearance there in 1749. The Duc de Luynes tells us in his reminiscences how greatly Louis XV. prized this artist and

admired his works. The Reader (p. 54) is a good example of the graceful, effortless manner in which Liotard was able to give the effect of a genre-painting to his portraits. The charming reader is Mademoiselle Lavergne, his niece, of whom he painted a portrait in 1752. His best-known work in this style is *la belle chocolatière*, called "The Chambermaid" (*die Kammerzofe*), in the Dresden Gallery.

The second foreigner, whom the French regard as the true reviver of their

No. 63.   Liotard.   *The Reader*

miniature art, is Peter Adolph Hall, a Swede (1736–1793). He had studied medicine at Upsala and Göttingen in accordance with his father's wishes, but soon decided to let medicine go by the board and devote himself to Art. He came to France in 1766 and by 1769 was Court painter. Handsome, musical and a good dancer, he won applause both for his appearance and his art. He married in 1771 Adelaide Bobin, whom he has charmingly portrayed with her son and daughter (p. 56). He was much in demand and earned from twenty to twenty-five thousand francs a year, a

sum his extravagant wife readily squandered. When the Revolution broke out and pleasure-loving Society had dwindled
away by emigration, Hall left France in 1791, without his
family. He died, sick, neglected and alone, at Lüttich in
1793. The Swedish master is entirely French in his perfection
of refined taste. He is unsurpassed in the art of giving warmth
and freshness to the complexion and liveliness to the eye;
he is equally suc-
cessful in repro-
ducing the light
touch of powder
on a rich wealth
of hair or the
sheen of silk, the
transparency of
muslin, many-
coloured ribbons
and artificial
flowers. The por-
trait of Madame
de Pompadour in
a frame set with
brilliants passed
from the Goncourt
collection into the
possession of
Pierpont Morgan.

No. 64. Hall. *Portrait of a Lady*

It must have been painted during the early days of the
artist's sojourn in Paris, for Louis XV.'s much-condemned
mistress died at the age of forty-two on 15th April, 1764.
To-day, when we most frequently call the eighteenth
century "the age of gallantry"—as if it had no other
characteristics than the immorality of a small section of
Society—the Pompadour is called in journalese the *grande
amoureuse*. Anyone who knows the age knows how untrue
this is. Jeanne Antoinette Poisson, wife of Lenormand
d'Etoiles, was devoured by the ambition to get to Court and

No. 65. Hall. *The Artist's Wife with Son and Daughter*

Isabey. *Princess Bagration*

Guérin. *General Kléber*

into Court Society; there was no question of love. When she
had attained this end and become Marquise de Pompadour
and mistress of the royal debauchee, her martyrdom began.
During the twenty years she was at Versailles, she had to
fight anew for her position every day and every hour. She had
scores of envious enemies and self-seeking friends, and the king's

No. 66. Hall. *Count Axel Oxenstierna*
Swedish Royal Collection

affection was her only support. If this affection had not yielded
to indifference on the king's part owing to the lady having
a fatal defect, who knows whether she could have held her
own for so long? So the king suffered her to remain because
he was used to her, and she had to rack her brains day by day
for ways of pleasing a man who was amused by nothing but
the coarsest sensuality.

The Pompadour's likeness was done at the commencement
of the artist's career; that of Queen Marie Antoinette during
his prime. The queen inherited the unlovely Habsburg

features of her mother, a large nose, thick lips and a heavy chin. But a Court painter knows no ugly princesses, and so the queen has become gracious and beautiful under Hall's brush. Joseph Boze alone dared to paint her faithfully. Marie

No. 67.   Unknown.
Mme de Pompadour

Antoinette could never be painted too often, for the Empress Maria Theresa continually plagued her for new pictures of herself, and scarcely wrote a letter without asking for one. She certainly did not fail to rebuke the queen severely when her too-fashionable dress displeased her; she demanded portraits of her in royal attire, not in negligée or male dress! The empress, who had grown up in the days of the laced bodice and hooped petticoat, condemned the tendency of fashion towards freedom of dress very severely (see, for example, Hall's portrait of an Unknown Lady (p. 60)), though she did not live to see the victory of the new mode.

In Hall's miniature of a woman artist (Plate V.) we see amongst a litter of studio accessories the harp, which began to appear in drawing-rooms at that time, and remained for more than a generation the favourite instrument of elegant Society. In the little genre-painting, The Kiss (p. 62), Hall shows his mastery of a piquant theme. The portrait of Princess Louise of Prussia (Plate VI.), painted by him at Aix-la-Chapelle in 1791, is one of his last. Princess Louise was the daughter of Prince Ferdinand, brother of Frederick the Great; she was born in 1770, and married Prince Anton Radziwill in 1796. She was gifted and clever, but not beautiful, being too stout and high-shouldered, and left some extraordinarily fascinating memoirs in which there is a great deal of interesting matter concerning the Prussian Court and Prince Louis Ferdinand, the princess's favourite brother. She was the mother of Princess Elisa Radziwill, who was so deeply beloved by the

Emperor William I. (as he afterwards became), though he dared not marry her. Princess Louise died in 1836 at Berlin, after a long and happy married life.

The golden age of French miniature art commences with Hall. When the miniature became a much-desired luxury in Society, artists of standing were obliged to devote themselves to its creation, and the Academy opened its doors to the miniaturists as it had to the historical painters. To be a member was not only an honour, but an indispensable condition, if a young artist wanted to make himself known; a painter who did not belong to the Academy had no other opportunity of exhibiting his work than in the so-called *Salon des Jeunes*, which was held on certain fête-days in the Place Dauphiné in the open air. To remedy this evil, one or two non-Academicians founded what we should call to-day a secession, the Academy of St. Luc, which exhibited paintings and miniatures by non-Academicians from 1751–1776. In 1776 the Academy, jealous of its opposition, had it closed.

No. 68. Hall. *Young Girl*

The *Exposition du Colisée*, which was started by the victims of too much discipline as compensation, only survived one season, and then the artists without the stamp of official recognition would have been once more without their exhibition had not La Blancherie founded the *Salon de la Correspondance* in 1779, in which any artist could exhibit on paying a membership subscription of two louis d'or. Quite in the modern fashion this salon of secessionists started a magazine, *Nouvelles de la République des Lettres*, in which exhibited works were dis-

No. 69.   Hall.   *Unknown Lady*

cussed. This adventure flourished until 1787 and then ended in financial disaster. In 1791 a *Salon des Artistes libres* was started in the rue Cléry, and finally, in 1793, the official salon was made accessible to all and the limiting privileges of the Academy removed.

Jean Baptiste Huet (1740–1810), a pupil of Leprince, and Degault, both contemporaries of Hall, owe their fondness for pastoral scenes (p. 62) to Rousseau's ideas. Gault, or Degault de St. Germain (1754–1842), is said to be the inventor of the miniature made in imitation of the cameo. The German, Johann Ernst Heinsius of Weimar, was Court painter at Paris to the daughter of Louis XV., and had a preference for antique and classical scenes (p. 63) in the fashionable manner. Pierre Chasselat (1753–1814) made charming little portraits with a slightly erotic flavour.

Jean Honoré Fragonard (1732–1806), a pupil of Boucher

and perhaps even more rococo, imparted to his miniatures the same piquant note of frivolity and *joie de vivre* as to all his other productions. His portrait of the actor Préville (p. 65) represents one of the most popular comedians of the French stage of the day. Pierre Louis Dubus, called Préville, made his début in 1753 at the age of twenty-two at the Comédie

No. 70. Jean Guérin. *Two Sisters*

Française, and became at once the favourite of public and authors alike. He retired from the stage in 1786, but came back for a short time when, in 1791, the theatre was in financial difficulties. In 1795 he suddenly lost his reason whilst acting, and died insane in 1799.

Antoine Vestier (1740–1810) is notable for the soft grey tones of his palette—almost like pastel. In 1789 he painted Latude, the celebrated Prisoner of the Bastille, who had languished there since the days of the Pompadour, having

No. 71. Unknown

simply been forgotten. In the Artist's Wife we have a characteristic costume portrait of Marie Anne Révérend, whom he married in 1764. She was the daughter of a painter in enamel, the wife of a miniature painter and the mother-in-law, through the marriage of her daughter Nicole in 1789, of another famous miniaturist, François Dumont.

François Campana (*d.* 1786) was appointed private painter to Queen Marie Antoinette, and was one of the artists who represented her in those peasant costumes or Amazonian riding-habits so despised by her mother. His pretty portrait of an Unknown Lady (p. 68) is very like an anonymous painting of the famous actress, Madame Favart (p. 68), as Babette, one of her most brilliant rôles. Marie Justine Benoite Duronceray came from

No. 72.   Hall.   *The Kiss*

Nancy to Paris in 1744, and in 1745 married Charles Paul Favart, director of the Opéra Comique. She bewitched the public by her charm and amiability. Marshal Moritz of Saxony (Marshal Saxe), son of Augustus the Strong and Countess Aurora von Königsmarck, was so enamoured that he pursued her everywhere and had her imprisoned by a *lettre de cachet* when she withstood the

No. 73.   Degault.
Shepherd and Shepherdess

No. 74. Heinsius. *Bacchante Crowning Statue of Pan*

importunate addresses of her tempestuous wooer. As he still did
not succeed, he swore he would have her husband killed unless
she became his mistress. Then she gave in at last, and was
only freed from her tenacious lover on his death in 1750.

Louis Lié-Périn (1753–1817) was the son of a cloth manu-
facturer of Reims and devoted himself to Art under the
guidance of Roslin at Paris. His Girl playing the Harp

No. 75.   Unknown

(p. 69) is a charming little
work and shows how effectively
the harp shows up a beautiful
arm. In 1799 the painter had
to give up his work and take
over his father's factory, which
he managed until his death.

Quite in the spirit of *Emile*
and the *Nouvelle Héloïse* is a
portrait of the children of the
Duc de Montesquiou (p. 70) by
Jacques Antoine Maria Lemoine
(1752–1824), a pupil of Maurice
Quentin de la Tour. The Duc
de Montesquiou-Fézensac was
President of the French National
Assembly in 1790 and died
in 1832.

The fashion of being seen
with small children, brought
about by Rousseau's teaching, is illustrated in the portrait of
Comtesse de Vaudreuil by Mathias (p. 71). The lady is the
wife of Joseph François de Paula, Comte Vaudreuil, who was
born in 1740 in San Domingo, entered the French army and
was on the staff of Soubise during the Seven Years' War.
He was made Governor of the Louvre in 1814 and died in 1817.

The various members of the Blarenberghe family have
quite a position of their own. Louis Nicolas, the father, Henri
Desiré, the son, Henri Joseph, the grandson—all excelled in
delicacy of workmanship. They have painted in the smallest

possible space scenes which are crowded with numerous—
one is tempted to say innumerable—figures. The Annual Fair
at St. Germain in 1763 is reckoned a marvel of their art, and
no less famous is the box which was
exhibited at the Congress of Vienna;
on the lid is painted the Marriage
Feast of Prince Charles de Rohan-
Rochefort, with hundreds of minute
figures. It is still in the possession
of the Rohan family. The Boccia
Players is in the collection of Pierpont
Morgan.

No. 76. Fragonard.
The actor Préville

Luc (Louis) Siccardi of Avignon
(1746–1825) came to Paris when young
and managed to retain the favour he
had earned at the Court of Louis XVI. through all vicissitudes. He
painted throughout the Direc-
tory, Empire and Restoration.
He painted Marie Tocqué,
who did her grandfather
Nattier good service by
giving her mother a help-
ing hand with his biography.
The Portrait of Two Chil-
dren on p. 73 was painted
in 1796 as a small me-
mento. Françoise du Plain
de Ste Albine was orphaned
through the death of both
her parents by the guil-
lotine. She was adopted by
her uncle, Pierre Boulou-
vard, and his wife, Madame
Jeanne Rose Allier de Haute-
roche. As a memento, the

No. 77. Hall. *Vicomte de Mortemart*
Collection Duc de Mortemart

parents by adoption had the little girl painted with their
own son Benoît. He died in 1803, barely twenty-two

years old, and the girl later married the Marquis de Pastour de Costebelle.

The miniaturist Dumont, Vestier's son-in-law, likewise survived the Revolution and the Empire. He had the extra-ordinary idea of currying favour at the Court of the Duchesse d'Angoulême by painting a portrait of Queen Marie Antoinette in a short-waisted Empire dress, as though that unhappy lady were still alive. The Duchess had the good.taste to ignore the painter and his work.

The whole world was ringing with the fame of Madame Vigée-Lebrun (p. 74). She had painted Court and Society at Paris, and left France on the outbreak of the Revolution, there being nothing for her to do there. She travelled Europe from south to north and painted nearly all the princesses

No. 78. Lagrenée. *Innocence in Danger*

there were between Naples and St. Petersburg. She herself claimed to have done more than 650 portraits. They are all, like the artist herself, graceful and charming. In addition to the numerous portraits we have of her, we get a speaking impression of her attractive personality from her reminiscences, which contain a description of her life. She died in Paris in 1842, aged eighty-seven. Vigée-Lebrun was one of those ladies who had had a passion for antiquity (even before the Revo-lution) and who occasionally dressed in Greek costume and held symposia in their houses. The portrait of Madame de Saint-Just, *née* Godart d'Ancourt (p. 75), shows the contrast between the merely graceful style and the stern antique Roman style which David brought into exclusive use. The wreath on her head and the harp in her hand show that this beautiful woman had literary aspirations. For quite a long time it was considered good form to be painted as Corinna; Augustin painted Madame Roberjot like this. With this artist we come to one of the most famous French miniaturists in the very midst of upheaval and the re-organisation of society.

Jean Baptiste Jacques Augustin, of Lorraine, came to Paris in 1781 at the age of twenty - two, and soon won himself a name as a painter of miniatures and enamels. He is distinguished for great freshness and originality of treat-ment. He is said to have painted about thirty miniatures before the Revolution, and to have made between five and six thousand francs. But it was during the Revolution that his fame and wealth be-came greatest and, a most exceptional fact, remained so under the Restoration likewise.

No. 79.   Vestier.   *Unknown Lady*

He painted Napoleon and Josephine, Eugène and Hortense Beau-harnais, the sisters and brothers-in-law of the Emperor, and, shortly afterwards, Louis XVIII., and the Duchesse d'Angoulême. His popularity grew to such a degree that where he had formerly received 200, 400 or 600 francs for a miniature, he was paid, at the time of the Restoration, 2000 to 3000 francs. He died in 1832 a victim of the first cholera epidemic. His wife, Pauline du Cruet, was originally a pupil of his, and became an excellent

No. 80.   Unknown.   *Mme Favart*

miniature painter under his guidance. As a memento of his marriage with her on the 20th of Messidor, in the eighth year of the Republic, he made a painting of his whole family. We see the artist himself, his mother, his wife and her relatives, Germain du Cruet, Madame du Cruet (*née* Cornus de la Fontaine), and Madame Rémondat (*née* du Cruet). This method of portraying several heads together was very popular; Dumont also painted himself and his relatives in this way.

The portrait of a lady known as Princess Lichnowski and that of a Young Woman at the Piano (Plate VII.) both belong to the eighteenth century. With the rest of his paintings we step into the new epoch. Mademoiselle Bianchi (Plate IX.) and Fanny Charrin (Plate VIII.) are dressed, as to hair and costume, in the style of 1800 under the Consulate; incredibly *décolletée* and in the most diaphanous muslin. The backgrounds are treated with unusual care, and are meant to be included in the characterisation. Fanny Charrin, herself

No. 81. Campana.   *Portrait of Unknown Lady*

a miniature painter, did not content herself with a mere allusion, but must have inscriptions to exhaust the list of her intellectual sympathies. She points a hand to the *Temple de l'amitié*, on the road to which is written *La Reconnaissance m'y conduit*, and on the entablature *Fanny en connaît tous les issues*. This must not be taken to mean that the poetical Fanny knew only the exits from the Temple of Friendship!

In Plate X. the artist has painted Mademoiselle Duchesnois as Sophonisba. She was one of the stars of the Paris stage, and during the Empire rivalled Mademoiselle Georges-Weymer. Catherine Josephine Rafin, called Duchesnois, made her début on 3 August, 1803, as Phèdre at the Théâtre Français,

No. 82.   Périn.   *Girl playing the Harp*

and delighted everyone by her expression and feeling. The public split into two camps, the adherents of Duchesnois and the adherents of Georges, which attacked each other with a rage and bitterness not easy to understand at the present day. The rivalry of the two tragediennes brought about the custom of the *claque*. Mademoiselle Duchesnois belonged to the élite of French actresses who played to a house of royal personages at Erfurt. Her star paled when the romantics Vigny, Hugo and Dumas drove classical tragedy off the stage for a number of years. She died in 1835 after having given the edifying spectacle of a reconciliation with the Church just before her death.

Caroline Murat (p. 78) was Napoleon's third sister and married Joachim Murat in 1800 at the age of eighteen. First Grand Duchess of Berg and later Queen of Naples, she had her part in the rise and fall of her family. Her husband was

No. 83.   Lemoine.   *Children of the Duc de Montesquiou*

shot at Pizzo on 13 October, 1815, after which she took the name of Countess Lipona and withdrew to her villa near Trieste, where she died in 1839.

The Duchess of Danzig (p. 79) is the "Madame Sans-Gêne" of Sardou's effective play which held the stage for so

Laurent. *Portrait*

Champmartin.   *Madame de Mirbel*

long. She was a laundress
and her husband, Fran-
çois Joseph Lefebvre,
the son of an Alsatian
miller. He received the
title in 1807 after the
capture of Danzig and
died in 1820, his twelve
sons and two daughters
having died before him.
Though the duchess
often convulsed the
Court by her speech and
behaviour, her private
life was unusually un-
troubled, and her
marriage happy; at her

No. 84. Mathias.
Comtesse de Vaudreuil and Child

death in 1835 at the age of seventy-six, she left to her nieces
property worth fifteen millions.

Countess Montalivet (p. 81) was the wife of Count Montalivet, who was Minister of the Interior in 1809, and died in 1823.
She was the mother of the other Minister of the same name, who
held his portfolio immediately after the Revolution of July,
that is, from 1830 to 1832. Before her marriage, when,

No. 85. Van Blarenberghe. *Scène galante.* Collection Monsieur Vauthier

as Mademoiselle Lauberie de St. Germain, she lived with her parents at Valence, Napoleon fell in love with her and wanted to marry her.

Another popular miniature-painter, only ten years younger than Augustin, was Jean Baptiste Isabey, whose long life (he died in 1855 at the age of eighty-eight) has been prettily called the diamond wedding of an artist and success. His career, described charmingly if not altogether truthfully in his autobiography, does indeed sound like a fairy tale. He started at the Court of Louis XVI. with portraits of the little Dukes of Berry and An-goulême, and finished when Napoleon III. and Eugénie were on the throne. During the Republic he became drawing-master at the institute of Madame Campan, where he came into touch with Hortense Beauharnais and her mother Josephine.

No. 86.   Siccardi.   *Unknown Lady*

Not only did he paint the Emperor and both the Empresses, he also had the arrangement of Court festivities, to which he had to impart an artistic *cachet*. He designed Marie Louise's dresses and, amidst all these distractions, managed to carry through such a course of work that it is almost impossible to believe that he really painted all the works which bear his name. During the Restoration he travelled through Europe and painted the fashionable world, his income at this time being from 40,000 to 50,000 francs a year. He had mastered every technique and even worked at the porcelain factory at Sèvres. It was he who made the famous table-top, one metre in diameter, with fourteen portrait of the Emperor and his marshals. This piece of works, for which Percier furnished the draft, was finished in 1810, and Isabey received 9000 francs for it. The whole table came to 35,000 francs and was in danger, on the return of the Bourbons, of being destroyed as unpatriotic. It was saved by accident. In 1903 this gorgeous piece of furniture was bought for 40,000 francs by Prince Ney de la Moskowa. Of a second and similar table we only have the design.

Isabey had designed a secretaire in 1811, from a plan of the celebrated architect Percier, which was to have numerous miniatures of the imperial family

No. 87.   Siccardi.   *Portrait of Two Children*

between strips of bronze gilt, painted on porcelain. However, it was probably never carried out,

Isabey's portrait of an Unknown Lady (p. 82) shows that he had tried to model himself on Plimer and Engleheart during a short visit to London at the end of the eighteenth century; but he soon developed his own manner.

His painting of Anne Françoise Lange (sometimes spelt L'Ange) represents one of the notorious beauties of the Directory dressed in that fashion (Plate XI.). She was an actress of quite mediocre gifts, but knew how to make the most of

F

her physical charms, and was famous for her liaisons and her prodigality. She was born in Geneva and very nearly died on the scaffold; she had good friends, however, who managed to find her shelter in a *maison de santé*, where she stayed until after the 9th of Thermidor. She was the mistress of Barras,

No. 88.   Dumont.   *Mme Vigée-Lebrun*

Mandrin and other influential men, and knew how to use her position for her own advantage. All Marie Antoinette's lace fell into her hands, amongst other things. In 1797, although only twenty-five years old, she grew so stout that she was obliged to retire from the stage. In 1799 Girodet painted her as Danaë and the shower of gold—a transparent allusion. She married a merchant of Brussels, Michel Jean Simons, and disappeared so utterly from *le monde où l'on s'amuse* that it is not even known exactly when she died.

On page 83 we see Napoleon when General Bonaparte;

No. 89. Dumont. *Mme de Saint-Just*

thin and with sharp, hard features, not yet the powerful Cæsar-like head of later days. It was by no means easy to satisfy the great man, however; Daru, the *Maréchal du Palais*, wrote to Isabey to say that Napoleon was not at all pleased with his portraits, he wanted to appear much handsomer. The portrait of the Empress Josephine (p. 83) was painted

No. 90. Signac. *Queen Ulrica Eleonora*. 1684
Swedish Royal Collection

in 1806, when this charming woman was at the height of her glory. But already shadows began to threaten the sunshine of her happiness, and a murmur of voices reminded Napoleon that an emperor should have an heir. When she was really divorced in December 1809 she bore her dismissal very badly, and suffered unutterably from the boredom to which her humble position reduced her. A halo of sentiment has been cast over the divorced Josephine by the ever-ready tongue of romance, but incorrectly. The Empress suffered far more from the straitened means which were forced upon her and her exile from Paris than from the separation from Napoleon. The Duchess of Dino relates that Louis XVIII. was scarcely in Paris before the ex-Empress besought an audience with him and, in a most undignified manner, begged to be received at Court.

The portrait of a Young Lady at the Piano (p. 84) probably dates from the first years of the nineteenth century. The Duchess of Ragusa (p. 85) was the wife of Marshal Marmont, who received his title for his government of Dalmatia

Gigola. *Duchess of Leuchtenberg*

Two Unknown Ladies

for many years. He
contributed to Napo-
leon's downfall when he
threw in his lot with the
Allies in 1814 and cut
off Napoleon's last hope
of recovery. Marmont
had to relate to the
young Duke of Reich-
stadt a history of the
whole life of his great
father — a proceeding
which extended over
several weeks and
earned the grateful
thanks of the unfor-

No. 91. Unknown

tunate youth. Marmont devoted his last years to compiling
his Memoirs,
which have be-
come an impor-
tant quarry of
information on
the history of the
First Empire. He
died in 1852, just
when the Empire
came to life again.

Isabey intro-
duced a new type
of fashionable
elegance in his
scarf-portraits, as
represented here
by Mrs. Damer
(p. 86) and Prin-
cess Bagration
(Plate XII.). He

No. 92. Augustin. *Mother and Child*

was the originator of this style of portraiture and painted dozens of ladies of the highest society between 1810 and 1820. Empresses and princesses, duchesses and *roturières*, all wanted to be painted in this romantic pose, languishing sentimentally as though they were only lent to the world for a moment and would soon spread their wings and float away in their gauzy veils to the cloud-capp'd towers. The Baroness du Montet writes in her *Reminiscences*: "Isabey has an unfailing method

No. 93.   Augustin.   *Caroline Murat*

for pleasing us—he is wildly flattering. No matter how ugly a woman may be, if *he* paints her she looks as fair and ethereal as a sylph." Princess Bagration is certainly a proof that all this soulfulness was only a matter of fashion, for she was completely of this world. She was Countess Catharine Skawronska, and married Field-Marshal Prince Bagration, eighteen years older than herself. He was not the only one to be favoured by her affections, however, for she was exceedingly generous in the bestowal of her love. Countess Lulu Thürheim, Comte de la Garde and others present at the festivities of the Vienna Congress, all describe the part played by the newly-widowed princess in the love intrigues of the day and place. She died in 1857. She was called "the lovely naked angel," on account of a certain lack of reserve in her attire. Forty years after this portrait was painted, when she was in her seventies, the lady was surprised by Baron Hübner in a tender and compromising situation.

No. 94. Augustin. *Duchess of Danzig: "Mme Sans Gêne"*

Jean Guérin (1760–1836) was Isabey's most important pupil, although seven years older than his master. He is a miniaturist of the very foremost rank, distinguished by powerful characterisation and a strength in his method of handling his brush most unusual in work of such small size. He was a painter and engraver and had engraved likenesses of the members of the National Assembly in 1789. When the mob stormed the Tuileries on 20 June, 1792, he was a soldier of the Garde Nationale, and is said to have saved the life of Marie Antoinette.

His portrait of Baroness de Fontette (p. 87) in Greek costume illustrates the taste of the day; the Dancer (p. 88) is an attempt to reproduce the classical style as made known by sketches from the frescoes of Herculaneum and Pompeii.

One of the La Vaupalière sisters (p. 61), whom he painted

in 1798, married Comte Langeron; the other the Marquis de Balleroy. The portraits of General Duhamel (p. 89), Comtesse Montangon (p. 90), an Unknown Lady (p. 91), prove the artist to possess a gift not often met with in miniaturists, namely, great strength in characterisation and the ability to create strongly-individualised portraits. Guérin's masterpiece is his portrait of General Kléber, a work not easily equalled in strength and passion, though of small size. The original is in the Louvre, which gave only 500 francs for it in 1849, but there are several replicas. Jean Baptiste Kléber of Strasburg chanced to become a pupil of the Munich Cadet Corps and entered the Austrian service in 1772. He left it in 1783 and became a building inspector at Belfort. In 1792 he joined the Republican army. His advance was rapid, and he was a general by the time he went to Egypt with Napoleon. On his murder in 1800 by a fanatical Mussulman at Cairo, Napoleon was freed from a secret adversary who might have been a source of danger to him, for Kléber was a Republican by strong conviction and determined to defend the Republic against the enemy within as well as the enemy without.

No. 95.   Augustin.   *Unknown Lady*

Side by side with the great masters of the art was a number of artists of the second rank. Of these is Charles Chatillon, who

No. 96. Augustin. *Countess Montalivet*

exhibited in the Salon from 1795–1808, and excelled in paintings made in imitation of cameos, a branch of the art invented by Degault, so it is said. His portrait of Napoleon (p. 92) in full dress and crowned with the imperial laurels gives the emperor the features he wished to have; in reality and according to impartial observers he was not like this. Caroline Pichler, who frequently saw him quite close at Schönbrunn in 1809, writes:

No. 97. Isabey. *Unknown Lady*

His appearance was not prepossessing. His features were regular, the chin particularly good, quite on antique lines, like the head of Antinous. But the fleshiness and too-great fullness of the face robbed these noble lineaments of the greater part of their nobility and significance.

Daniel Saint (1778–1847), a pupil of Isabey, approached his master so closely that the latter frequently signed his productions and let them pass for his own. Saint is supposed to have painted the miniature of Napoleon that he sent his bride in a setting of brilliants costing 175,000 francs. To-day the medallion is in the possession of Countess Thérèse Fries, but the diamonds are now replaced by paste. According to Leo Schidlof, however, the painter was Duchesne, not Saint. The portrait of Princess Pauline Borghese fully justifies the artist's fame. She was Napoleon's beautiful and famous sister, and made the most modest alliance of all his relations.

She married first General Leclerc and then, when a young widow, Prince Camillo Borghese in 1803; he received the title of Duke of Guastalla in 1806. She died at Florence in 1825. No traveller passes through Rome without stopping to admire Canova's statue of her at the Villa Borghese.

No. 98.   Isabey.
Napoleon Bonaparte

Jean Antoine Laurent (1763–1832) was much patronised by the Beauharnais family. His charming Unknown Lady (Plate XIV.), painted in 1804, is of the young wife of one of General Rapp's adjutants. Laurent kept in favour with Louis XVIII. and Charles X. also. At the age of sixty-nine he was awarded the Légion d'Honneur by Louis Philippe, and died of joy at this unexpected honour.

Marie Nicolas Ponce-Camus (1778–1839) was a pupil of David. His portrait of a Young Lady in 1800 (p. 94) illustrates the style of coiffure known as *coup de vent*.

A portrait of Napoleon's mother (p. 96) after Gérard belongs to the class of miniatures by artists more or less connected with the Court. Maria Lätitia Ramolino, born in 1750 and married to Carlo Bonaparte in

No. 99.   Isabey.   *Empress Josephine*

1767, became a widow in 1785 and died at Rome in 1836. She beheld her children rise through poverty and need to sit on the most ancient thrones of Europe, a destiny that nowise perturbed her serenity of temperament. "Pourvou que ça doure," she remarked sceptically in her Franco-Italian *charabia* when told of some new glory that her house had won. She was always Madame Mère, the thrifty housewife who had learnt the value of money and never spent it on luxuries except when she bought the relics for which, as a bigoted Catholic, she had a great weakness. The painting here called Napoleon as a Boy (p. 96), if it represents any member of the family at all, must be of Napoleon III. or the Duke of Reichstadt. When Napoleon I. was a boy, children of both sexes were dressed as to hair and clothes exactly like grown people, and suitably comfortable dress for children did not come into use until the first Napoleon was a grown man.

No. 100.   Isabey.   *Young Woman at the Piano*

François Huet Villiers (1772–1813), like so many of his more important contemporaries (Gérard and David, to name only two), painted Juliette Récamier's renowned loveliness. She was the daughter of a Lyons banker named Bernard, born in 1777 and, at fifteen, married the banker Jacques Récamier in Paris. During the Directory she was the leader of Paris Society. Reichardt, who visited Paris at that time, sent

home enthusi-
astic accounts
of her appear-
ance, her house
and her circle
of friends. Na-
poleon could
not bear her
and declined to
help her hus-
band when his
business got
into difficulties
and he had to
go into liquida-
tion. So the
beautiful and
elegant woman
withdrew from
Society. "The
most beautiful
woman of her
time" was as
cold as ice and
her virtue was
said to be a

No. 101.   Isabey.   *Duchess of Ragusa*

matter of necessity. Napoleon, Prince Augustus of Prussia
and many others sued for her love in vain. The friends of her
heyday maintained that the fair Juliette's charms had not
withered, but the younger generation was less indulgent.
"I thought Madame Récamier a perfect little goose," writes
Charles de Rémusat in 1816 to his mother, and Gavarni, who
met her at the salon of the Duchess of Abrantès, thought
the "plump little woman" looked quite an ordinary country
bumpkin. The day of a beautiful woman is indeed brief, and
she is fortunate who does not outlive her renown as did the
lovely Juliette. She died in 1849 of cholera.

Pierre Paul Prudhon (1758–1823), the painter who fared so ill because his graceful art did not accord with the taste of the day for the stern Roman virtues of a David, painted Constance Mayer la Martinière (p. 97), his unlucky friend. Prudhon had made a hasty marriage in his youth and was tied to a semi-insane wife who finally went quite mad, but from whom he could not free himself. Constance eased his lot by consenting to live with him, and they were both happy and contented, in spite of poverty, until calumnies and slights of various kinds drove the poor girl to her death. She poisoned herself in 1821, and Prudhon pined away and died only two years after her. She was a gifted miniature-painter, as her portrait of Madame Roland shows. Jeanne Marie Philipon married Roland de la Platière, an official of the old Monarchy, in 1780. She became an enthusiastic Republican and influenced her husband so that he came over to the side of the new Government and became Minister of the Interior in 1792. When the Girondists, to whose party she belonged, succumbed to the attacks of the Mountain in June 1793, she was imprisoned and went to the guillotine

No. 102.   Isabey.   *Mrs. Damer*

No. 103. Guérin. *Baroness de Fontette, Marquise de Tilly d'Orceau*

on 9 November, not yet forty years of age. Her husband managed to escape, but killed himself a week later. This gifted and industrious lady employed her leisure in prison in writing her memoirs, thus supplying us with a valuable document for the understanding of a rare personality and a stormy age.

No. 104.   Guérin.   *Girl Dancing*

We must include Alexander Kucharski (1741–1819) amongst French artists, for he lived and studied in Paris, though he was born at Warsaw. He painted Marie Antoinette in the Temple and the Conciergerie shortly before her death, and also her unhappy second son, whom history ironically calls Louis XVII. The unfortunate child, who died at the age of ten from the brutal ill-treatment of the shoemaker Simon, his so-called "master," was the cause of much interest later on, by reason of a number of false Dauphins, each declaring himself to be the little prince and to have been secretly rescued from the Temple. The first of these pretenders was Jean Marie Hervagault, a tailor; the second Mathurin Bruneau, a shoemaker; the third a watchmaker of Spandau, Karl Wilhelm Naundorf; the fourth Louis Hebert, an adventurer; the fifth a Russian major, Ludwig Carlowitsch de Ligny-Luxemburg, etc., etc. Naundorf played his part the longest and with most

Two Unknown Duchesses of the House of Habsburg

Füger.   *Gentleman in a Brown Coat*

success, in spite of the fact that his antecedents were known and that he had already made acquaintance with the prison at Brandenburg. He was used by Fronde the legitimist as a battering-ram against Louis Philippe during the July Monarchy, and supported by wealthy members of the nobility who could not themselves have believed in his story. The so-called duke did not even understand a word of French when he appeared in Paris in 1832, and never lost his German accent even after he had learnt the language.

It is doubtful whether the great Spaniard, Goya, should be credited with the production of miniatures, particularly as we know that he suffered from eye trouble; but the portrait of Queen Marie Louise of Spain (p. 103), if not actually by him, is certainly copied from a painting of his. Goya made innumerable portraits of that queen with the lovely body and common face; there is a portrait of her in the same uniform as in this miniature, but on horseback, at the Prado in Madrid. She was the daughter of

No. 105. Guérin.
General Duhamel

the Duke of Parma, born in 1751, and married Carlos, afterwards King Carlos IV. of Spain, in 1765. After changing her lovers as easily as most people change their clothes, she became so violently attached to a handsome guardsman that she heaped honours, dignities and titles upon him and finally had him made Prince of the Peace. The hatred with which she pursued her eldest son, later Ferdinand VII., led to the deplorable catastrophe of 1808, when Napoleon drove out the Spanish royal family *en bloc* and made his brother Joseph King of Spain. The trio, Carlos IV., Marie Louise and Don Manoel Godoy, Principe de la Paz, withdrew to Rome. They were inseparable and did not return to Spain

G

even after the Restoration. Marie Louise died at Rome in 1819, and on 15 January Gabriele von Humboldt writes: "The remains of the queen had to be kept in Rome for a whole week; 12,000 Masses were said for her. She will be *per forza spedita nell paradiso.*" If heaven allowed such

No. 106.   Guérin.   *Comtesse Montangon*

saints as these to "creep and intrude," there would be merry doings indeed there!

The great period of miniature art comes to an end when lithography begins to make headway. This art, German in origin, grew to maturity first of all in France, and was quickly raised to the height of perfection by gifted French artists. The lithographic stone is a substance that can be worked

with quill, etching-tool or wash with equal success, and easily
provides the most striking effects. Portrait-lithography ousted
the miniature with its laborious technique, and only a few
stragglers remained faithful to the great tradition and passed
it on to a less appreciative generation. The most gifted of these
was Louis François Aubry (1770–1850), a pupil of Isabey
and painter of the Lady with the Harp (p. 104) in 1817.

We cannot suffi-
ciently deplore the
fact that the name
of his model is not
known. The elegant
setting, the expen-
sive and choice
attire, the splendid
shawl, which alone
represents an enor-
mous sum, all
suggest a lady of
quality; whilst the
peculiar expression
reminds us of the
Duchesse de Berry,
who married in
1816, and one of
whose peculiarities
was a cast in one
eye.

No. 107.   Guérin.   *Unknown Lady*

Madame de
Mirbel (Plate XV.) was the most popular miniature-painter
under Charles X. and Louis Philippe. Aimée Zoé Lizinka
Rue was a pupil of Augustin and made a sensation at Court
by painting a speaking likeness of Louis XVIII. without
having had a single sitting from the king. She was made
painter to the king and married Charles François Brisseau
de Mirbel in 1823. She died of cholera in 1849, aged fifty-three.
Her miniature of the two sisters Pourtalès (p. 105) must have

been painted about the year 1830 and represents two ladies of a noble family of Swiss origin, which bore the title of count both in France and Prussia. Members of their family have played as great a rôle in the diplomacy of both countries as in Parisian Society, where Countess Pourtalès had one of the most brilliant of the salons under the Second Empire. Fanny Charrin, of Lyons, was a pupil of Augustin also. She painted at the porcelain works at Sèvres and was admired for her excellent miniatures carried out in the graceful manner of Isabey (p. 107). She died in Paris in 1854.

No. 108. Chatillon. *Napoleon I.*

Frédéric Millet (1786–1859) was a pupil of Isabey and Aubry. He was one of the last of the miniature-painters and made portraits of many of the members of the English aristocracy. His portrait of Lady Hargreaves (p. 108) represents one of those languishing English drawing-room beauties in the manner in which they were depicted in those days in keepsakes, albums of beauties and similar publications.

We must include Giovanni Battista Gigola of Brescia amongst French artists, because he received his training as a painter in enamel and miniatures in Paris. Plate XVI. represents the Duchess Augusta Amalia von Leuchtenberg, wife of Eugène Beauharnais, Napoleon's stepson. He was Viceroy of Italy and hoped to receive the throne of Poland from his stepfather. The fall of the Emperor put an end to his dreams and he had to content himself with the title of Prince of Eichstätt. Eugène died in 1824 and his widow, daughter of King Max of Bavaria, lived until 1851. The little girl is Josephine, Princess of Bologna, who married the Crown Prince Oscar of Sweden and died a queen and widow in 1876. Her brothers and sisters also made brilliant marriages, thanks to their great beauty. One brother, through his marriage to Donna Maria da Gloria, became King of Portugal; another, through his marriage with the youngest daughter of Czar Nicholas I., became Grand Prince of Russia; one sister became Empress of Brazil, and another Princess of Hohenzollern-Hechingen. Gigola died at Milan in 1841.

THE GERMAN SCHOOL

GERMAN miniature art, like that of England and France, originated in the sixteenth century. The reason why it did not reach such perfection in Germany as in the other two countries, lies in the fact that there was no German Court at which this luxurious art could develop. There was no central Court life

No. 109.   Ponce-Camus.   *Young Girl*

in Germany as there was under the last Valois in Paris or the last Tudors in London.

Germany had miniature-artists of the first rank, but they laboured in obscurity; in twofold obscurity indeed.

Hans Mülich (1516–1573), to whom Ernst Lemberger has recently drawn attention, worked in Munich at a small but intellectual Court, and though this alone sufficed to withhold his production from a wider circle, the fact of his having painted his portraits in books made them even more inaccessible. Some belong now to the treasures of the Royal Hof- und Staatsbibliothek at Munich, and their rich and costly style must have prevented them from being much used or known.

The two Ostendorfers, father and son, were also among the miniature-painters at the Court of the Dukes of Bavaria, and were employed as book-illuminators, the one at the beginning, the other in the second half, of the sixteenth century. The great artists of the period also—Dürer, Cranach, etc.—produced portraits of very small size, though they cannot on that account be reckoned as true miniatures.

The contents of the Brandenburg Kunstkammer (known to older visitors of Berlin art-collections at the Palace and later at the New Museum) were divided, about a generation ago, between the Hohenzollern Museum and the Kunstgewerbe Museum, and included a miniature of the Margrave Frederick the Elder of Anspach, painted on silver and ascribed to Dürer.

Book-illuminations of Glockendon and others went forth from Dürer's workshop, but we can only guess how far the master himself had a hand in them. On the other hand the workshop of Lucas Cranach (1472–1553) was prolific of everything that was within the scope of a painter, and paintings, drawings, woodcuts and the like were produced almost as if from a factory. This explains the stiffness and lack of soul of so many of the productions which are signed with the Dragon —the sign of the Cranach workshops.

No. 110.   Saint.   *Lady with Veil*

Cardinal Albrecht von Brandenburg (p. 109) was the son of the Electoral Prince Johann Cicero and became Electoral Prince of Mainz at the age of twenty-four. He was a great art-lover and had himself painted by Dürer and Cranach, ordered Peter Vischer to make his tomb, and used to buy the paintings of Grünewald, Hans Baldung Grien and others. The Court he held at Halle on the Saal was one of the most brilliant of the day. On the occasion of the visit of the Elector

No. 111.   Unknown.   *Napoleon as a Boy*

Joachim II. of Brandenburg and his wife at Easter in 1536, the cardinal spent 50,000 guilders in fourteen days and gave in addition presents to the value of 100,000 guilders.

Two hundred years later a prince of this type would have spent his money on building a palace or making a collection of Italian pictures. The cardinal did, however, try his hand at architecture when he founded the cathedral—the so-called Neues Stift at Halle. He furnished all the churches magnificently and brought together a treasure-house of relics which could stand comparison in rarity and in costliness of the shrines with the famous collection of Frederick the Wise at Wittenberg. The teaching of Luther was already spreading over North Germany, whilst Albrecht was trying to bolster up the old faith by means of the most resplendent ceremonials and stately processions. Two factors helped to bring all this magnificence to an end—

No. 112.   Gérard.
Mme Bonaparte, Mother of Napoleon

debts and the Reformation. Even the cardinal's huge means became exhausted, his debts became immense, and even the Fuggers would lend no more. It is known that Tetzel sold indulgences for the cardinal and was accompanied by Fugger's agents, who took their proportion of the pennies of the credulous from him the moment they were paid. The cardinal's finances

No. 113. Prudhon.
Sketch for a Miniature of Constance Mayer

could no longer bear the drain of the Neucs Stift; and on 22 March, 1541, the last Mass was read there and the costly jewels and sacred bones were pledged or sold. The Reformation took possession of the town. Albrecht died in 1545.

Barthel Bruyn (*c.* 1493–*c.* 1556), a Rhenish painter, was a contemporary of the Saxon Cranach. He came from Cologne and was a pupil of the master who painted the Death of the Virgin. He is famous for his altar-pieces. He seems to have

also painted very small pictures, as his Portrait of a Lady
(p. 110) shows. Although we do not know the name of the
lady, the picture is of great interest as it is, according to
Lemberger, the earliest miniature known in West Germany.

No. 114.   Isabey.   *Portrait of Aubry*
Collection Monsieur Coblentz

At the be-
ginning of the
seventeenth cen-
tury we hear of
Friedrich Brentel
(1580–1651), who
was equally suc-
cessful with
engraving or
miniature-paint-
ing. The Grand
Duke's Kupfer-
stichkabinett
(Print Room) at
Karlsruhe con-
tains a number
of portraits by
him of members
of the Solms
family.

After this,
German art
suffered a long
stagnation owing
to the frightful
misery caused by
the Thirty Years' War. The Courts grew accustomed to giving
orders for any artistic work to foreigners—Dutch and French
in the North of Germany, Italian in the South.

The two beautiful miniatures of Noble Ladies (Plate XVII.)
belong to this time; they are in the National Museum at Munich
and must have been painted about the year 1640.

Jean Pierre Huault, a Frenchman, worked in enamel at

the Court of the Elector of Brandenburg. In 1691 he received an annuity of 400 thalers, for which he had to deliver two miniatures a year. At the same time the German enamel-worker, Lorenz Eppenhoff, received 300 thalers, 100 less than the Frenchman, and had to produce six pictures a year. Samuel Blesendorf was a pupil of Huault and distinguished himself in enamel-work, engraving and oil-painting. He died in 1706 in Berlin.

At the Bavarian Court, after the marriage of the Elector Ferdinand Maria with Princess Adelaide of Savoy, Italian influence predominated, but under his son, the Elector Max Emanuel (p. 111), French influence came to the fore. This prince, during whose reign Bavaria went through grievous times, began to govern at the age of seventeen in 1679, and in 1685 married the Archduchess Marie Antoine of Austria, daughter of the Emperor Leopold. He became a widower in 1692, and then married Princess Thérèse Kunigunde Sobieska, daughter of the Polish king who had delivered Vienna in 1683. Max Emanuel's eldest son was to have come to the Spanish throne after Charles II.'s death, but died suddenly at Brussels. Whether the stupidity of his physicians sufficed to bring about his end, or whether, as the Duchess of Orleans, better known as Liselotte, maintained, an Austrian dose facilitated matters, will never be determined. At any rate the Elector entered the War of the Spanish Succession on the French side and thus brought upon his unhappy country all the horrors of an invasion and government by Austria.

Whilst his wife was enjoying the pleasures of Venice and his children were harshly treated in captivity by his adversary, the Elector passed the years of banishment at Versailles with more cheerfulness than dignity, as the Duchess of Orleans frequently informs us. He was re-established in dignities and lands and died in 1726.

It cannot, unfortunately, be ascertained precisely who are the ladies, presumably princesses, of the House of Habsburg on Plate XVIII. Since their hair is dressed in the style known as "the fontange" they must have been painted between the years 1685 and 1714, for that was about the length of time this style of coiffure beautified and oppressed the heads of fashionable ladies. It must have been no easy matter to balance this erection on the head, for it was far more complicated than

No. 115.   Isabey.   *Louise, Queen of Belgium*
Collection La Duchesse de Vendôme

it looked. The Duchess of Orleans used to laugh at her own "fontange," which was always on one side, and indeed the weight must have been considerable, for the hair and pins, slides and all sorts of ornaments were piled on a framework; a witty Parisian abbé once remarked that ladies had their locks dressed by locksmiths.

The best-known German miniaturist of the first half of

the eighteenth century is Balthasar Denner (1685–1748), the artist of the Hansa towns. He was born in Hamburg, educated at Danzig and died at Rostock. The regard which was once paid him by princes and nobles is now offered by that part of the public which is compelled by the force of education to visit the picture-galleries. His art of wrinkles and pores, which leaves out no hair or pucker, always delights all those who confuse art with artistry. His well-known (must one say famous, dare one say infamous?) heads of an old man and an old woman were more surrounded at the old Pinakothek at Munich than even the Van der Werffs; if Tschudi had spared them, who knows whether his brilliant re-arrangement of the gallery would have met with so much opposition? The Courts of Germany gave Denner quantities of commissions. He received twenty thalers for a bust-portrait and forty if the hands showed (pp. 112, 113).

Daniel Chodowiecki (1726–1801) has always received most appreciation for his charming engravings of Prussia at the time of Frederick the Great, but he devoted the greater part of his life to miniature-painting. While still a child at Danzig, he painted dozens of small portraits of Stanislaus Lesczynski, the Polish king. He went to Berlin with the intention of entering the business of his uncle, Anton Ayrer. It was a hardware and fancy goods business, and he worked at miniatures and enamels there for many years until he had made himself independent, though he continued to work at this branch of his art. Frederick the Great and Chodowiecki are inseparably linked together. The little Berlin painter earned a marvellous income out of the Prussian king's renown (for years he produced enough portraits of his king to earn 100 thalers a month); on the other hand the artist faithfully preserved for his own day and for posterity the features, mien and appearance of "old Fritz." His portraits were much more convincing and characteristic than those of Pesne the Court painter. Frederick never sat to Chodowiecki, who himself humorously relates how he had proof of Frederick's distaste when on a visit at Sans Souci. Meyer, a modeller from the porcelain factory, arrived with a finished bust of the king and begged to be allowed to correct it "from nature." Frederick ordered him to be refused and to be told to find an old ape and to correct his bust by its grimaces, the likeness was sufficient! Although the artist never had actual sittings from the king he saw him often enough to be able to imprint a characteristic picture of him on his imagination. Chodowiecki made portrait busts of Frederick the Great, and also painted his portrait on horseback and gave his conceptions such an undeniable stamp of truth that posterity sees Frederick as Chodowiecki saw him.

No. 116.   Millet.   *Unknown Lady*

This artist was master of all the technique of miniature-painting, and could work in enamel, oil, watercolour, etc. He was considered dear in his own day, for he asked from fifteen to fifty thalers a painting, according to the time and labour expended on it—usually twenty-five to thirty thalers. He charged fifteen to twenty thalers for heads in enamel, forty thalers for very small miniatures such as were worn in rings or trinkets, and eight louis d'or for bracelet miniatures.

There worked at this time at Dresden a mad fellow called Gabriel Ambrosius Donath, who had all sorts of whims and crotchets and wore a long beard, like Liotard. The Mengs

Füger. *Princess Elizabeth Wilhelmina Louisa.*

Füger.   *Countess Merveldt*

family also belongs to this time. Ismael Mengs (1688–1764) was a Dane who excelled in miniature-work and trained his whole family—his son Anton Raphael and his daughters Julie and Thérèse—in the same art. Raphael Mengs (1728–1779), who exercised as much influence on the Continent as did his contemporary Reynolds in England, has done great work in miniature and pastel, and with more success perhaps than with oils or fresco. His sister, Thérèse Maron (1725–1806), also excelled in this technique. She taught Maria Cosway and, like her, died in a convent.

No. 117. Goya.
Queen Marie Louise of Spain

Anton Graff, a painter who, in an artificial age, had the gift of preserving a fresh and natural note in his portraits, and Adam Friedrich Oeser, both did miniature-work.

Many other artists, whose aspirations, perhaps, went farther, had to earn their daily bread by the painting of miniature-portraits.

Jakob Asmus Carstens lived from 1783–1788 in Lübeck, where he devoted himself to the art of the miniature. The Weimar Museum possesses twenty-three drawings in pencil by him, which are considered "excellent and striking."

Philipp Otto Runge, whose harsh and powerful work was appreciated by subsequent generations, began his artistic career with the drawing of miniature-portraits in pencil. No. 127 on p. 115 is one of his early attempts.

Doris Stock (1761–1815), the aunt of Theodor Körner,

belonged to the Dresden set. Her portrait of Goethe's famous friend (p. 116), Frau von Stein, shows this much-talked-of lady in her prime and with the quantity of hair demanded by fashion. No woman need envy her her coiffure, for no hair ever grew naturally in such luxuriance and elegance. Wigs are the explanation of the apparent luxuriance of hair at this period. They were made no secret of, and frequently one of a different colour would be worn in the evening or to go with a different dress. This also explains why we frequently find in portraits at this period that the same lady has different-coloured hair; for instance, Queen Louise appears in auburn, *blond cendré* or light brown hair. Charlotte von Schardt was born in 1742 and in 1764 married the Grand Master of the Horse (von Stein), became a widow in 1793, and died in 1827. Her tragedy was, not that she lost the affection of Goethe after she had had it for ten years, but that she was forced to live down this loss for forty years in close proximity to the once-loved one. It was that which made her so bitter and malicious in her old age and sharpened her tongue against him and his.

No. 118.   Aubry.   *Lady with a Harp*

All the artists already mentioned were good miniature-

painters, but the hey-day of this art was reached at the end
of the eighteenth century and in Vienna.

At the Court there had always been miniaturists—the
charming little painting of the Emperor Joseph II. is a good
example. It is in a silver-gilt pendant set with emeralds and
rubies. The emperor was born in 1741 and the portrait shows
him still young and full of the wild ideas with which he tried
to benefit his
people. When he
died in 1790 at
the age of forty-
nine he was a
broken, discon-
tented man, who
confessed that he
had achieved
nothing of all
that he had aimed
at. He had, in-
deed, as Frede-
rick the Great
said of him,
always been too
precipitate.

Liotard was a
long time in
Vienna, and en-

No. 119. Mme de Mirbel. *Mlles de Pourtalès*

joyed the favour of the Empress Maria Theresa, but he was
not so much the product of the great period of Viennese
miniature art as was the Swabian, Heinrich Friedrich Füger.
He was born at Heilbronn in 1754, studied at first under
Nicolas Guibal in Ludwigsburg, and then under Oeser in
Leipzig. He visited Vienna in the suite of the English
ambassador to Dresden, Sir Robert Murray Keith, and
settled there in 1774. Prince Kaunitz procured him an
allowance, with which he went to Italy and studied there;
on his return in 1783 he was made Sub-Director of the
H

Academy, and in 1795 Director. In 1806 he became Director of the Imperial Picture Gallery, and died in 1818.

Füger stands in a place apart as a miniaturist. He has never been excelled either by predecessors or successors, scarcely even equalled, and Leisching is perfectly right when he says of the Cavalier in the Brown Coat (Plate XIX.): "Amongst his contemporaries, even in England and France, there is none who could have done better than this." In artistic sensibility Füger stands out from Cosway or Hall, and surpasses them, moreover, in his gift for individuality of conception. The strength of his characterisation has saved his miniatures from that monotony which so spoils Cosway's work. In 1798 Füger's eyes obliged him to give up miniature-work. He devoted himself henceforth to that type of classical historical picture which David had made the fashion, but though he covered many square yards of canvas he never reached the standard of his miniatures and remained, as has often been said, great in small things, small in great.

The Court and aristocracy took him up enthusiastically, and their commissions produced some of his most brilliant performances.

Maria Theresa (p. 118) was painted by him with some of her children. The Empress is wearing the widow's weeds which she never discarded after her husband's death in 1765. Behind her chair stands her son, the Emperor Joseph II.; on the extreme left is her favourite daughter Maria Christine, married in 1766 to Duke Albert of Sachsen-Teschen, who is seen beside her. In the background the unmarried children are crowded together—the Archduke Maximilian, Grand Master of the Teutonic Order, the last Elector of Cologne, who was driven out of his kingdom and died in 1801 in his old home. Next to him is the Archduchess Maria Anna, abbess of the convent at Prague, and Archduchess Maria Elizabeth, abbess of the convent at Innsbruck. These ladies had a life of dismal bore-dom at Court. Once the Archduchess Maria Anna had to undergo a slight operation for a swelling on her back. On being commiserated with by the English ambassador she replied: "Pray do not begrudge me this slight distraction, for I have no other."

Princess Wilhelmine Louise (Plate XX.) was the first of

No. 120. Fanny Charrin. *Portrait of a Lady*

the four wives of the Emperor Francis I. She was a daughter of Duke Friedrich Eugen von Württemberg and born in 1767. She married in 1788 and died in 1790 in child-bed, only a few days before the Emperor Joseph II.

The Archduchess Marie Clementine (p. 119), born in 1777, married the then Crown Prince, afterwards King Francis I,

No. 121.   Millet.   *Lady Hargreaves*

of Sicily, in 1797. She died in 1801. The Archduchess Marie
Christine (p. 120) was the daughter of the Emperor Francis I.
and Maria Theresa. She was born in 1742 and married to
Duke Albert of Sachsen-Teschen in 1766. She was Statthälterin
of the Netherlands and, after the House of Habsburg had lost
this inheritance, lived with her husband in Vienna. Caroline
Pichler in her Memoirs praises her for her "noble mien,
intellectual expression and well-chosen attire," the last in
striking contrast to that of the Archduchess Marie Louise, then
the wife of Napoleon. The Archduchess died in 1798 and her
husband in 1822. He was much loved by the imperial family and
is not forgotten to-day in the famous art collection known as
the Albertina, which he founded. The Archduke Joseph Anton

Johann (p. 120) was Count Palatine of Hungary, and his first wife was a Russian grand-duchess—the only example of an alliance between the Catholics of Lorraine and the Greek-Catholic Holstein-Gottorps. He died in 1847, the year of the great rising in Hungary.

Füger's best-known work is his portrait of the three Countesses Thun to which Laban attached so much im-portance in his researches on Füger and on which he laid stress in relation to his theory of the importance of this artist as a minia-turist. The por-trait was painted in 1788 and repre-sents the three daughters of Count Thun-Hohenstein-Klösterle, a man strongly attracted by the mystic school of thought that was growing up in the second

No. 122.   Cranach the Elder.
Cardinal Albrecht of Brandenburg

half of the eighteenth century in the reaction against the scepticism and rationalism everywhere rife. He was a dreamer, a Rosicrucian and a follower of Mesmer, who was in Vienna at that time trying to restore the sight of the blind Therese von Paradeis. The Count also tried to effect marvellous cures as his master did. The daughters, here seen kneeling before an altar *"sacré à l'amitié,"* were famous beauties and all made brilliant matches. Elizabeth, the eldest, born in 1764, married Count Andreas Kyrillowitsch Razumowski, a Russian diplomat, who was ambassador successively to Copenhagen, Stockholm, Naples and Vienna, but spent the greater part of his life in Vienna, where he built himself a noble palace in the Landstrasse. He was known in Society, on account of his numerous adventures, as the Russian Lovelace. His wife was not very happy with him, for he only tolerated her, whilst she loved him passionately. Count Roger de Damas, who was deeply and vainly in love with her, has in his Memoirs described a six weeks' journey he made in the autumn of 1806 from Palermo to Trieste to accompany his friend, who was extremely ill, to Vienna. They had to pass through the enemy fleet, which was in occupation of the Adriatic. The Countess died on 23 December, 1806.

No. 123.   Bruyn.   *Unknown Lady*

The second sister, Christine, was born in 1765, married Prince Carl Lichnowski in 1788, and through her son became the grandmother of Prince Felix, who was murdered in 1849 in France. She seems to have been somewhat of a saint, and Countess Lulu Thürheim reports strange things of her.

She had twinges of conscience [writes the Countess] which made her think that her coldness had alienated her husband's affection. She did not love him, yet she carried her advances to the extent of once enticing him into a house of ill-fame where, to his indignation, he recognised his own wife! Nevertheless the poor woman was never unfaithful to her husband, though he would easily have forgiven her; that cynical and dastardly libertine well deserved to be cuckolded.

Füger.   *Unknown Lady*

Füger.   *Count Platon Subow* (?)

Beethoven dedicated several of his works to this lady. She died in 1841. The youngest sister, Marie Caroline, born in 1769, married in 1793 Richard Clanwilliam, later Lord Guildford of Guillhall, and died in 1800. Her children, especially Richard, "with most beautiful brown eyes," play a great part in the amusing Memoirs of Countess Thürheim.

Countess Marie Therese Pergen (Plate XXI.) was born in 1763, married Count Merveldt in 1784, and died in 1802.

It is a pity that in the case of so many of Füger's portraits it is not known whom they represent. This is all the more to be regretted as these unknown persons, the Man with a Letter for instance (p. 123), and many ladies, always have such strongly individualised features that one would be interested to know who they are. On p. 124, an unknown lady with a classic profile attracts us by her charm, the half-length Portrait of

No. 124.   Unknown.
Max Emanuel, Electoral Prince of Bavaria

a Lady in full dress by her melancholy fragility of aspect (Plate XXII.). Her costume belongs to the end of the seventeen-eighties, and the large ruffle and puffed sleeves give a knightly effect, for it was the time when the romantic novels and plays of Benedict Naubert, Spiess, etc., were the fashion, and people sought in the age of chivalry for great heroism and the sturdier virtues. Füger also painted several gentlemen of the Austrian nobility with the characteristics of the chivalric age, especially the large ruff of the sixteenth and seventeenth centuries.

Count Bellegarde, Count Esterhazy, Field-Marshal Laudon and others were done in this way. In 1793 Bethman, the actress, introduced the large ruffs to Berlin, where they became the fashion, and ten years later they were worn in state as *chérusses* at the coronation of Napoleon and Josephine. It is uncertain whether the Man in the Red Coat (Plate XXIII.) is Count Platon Subow or, as seems more likely, Prince Jus-

No. 125.   Denner.   *Old Man*

sopoff; there is a certain resemblance between Füger's portrait and one of Subow painted by Lampi and engraved by James Walker. He was the last of Catherine II.'s many favourites and was all the more beloved by her as he possessed, in addition to the essential physical advantages, gifts of mind such as the Empress was not accustomed to find in her favourites.

J. Grassi (1757–1838) is one of those artists whose work is contemporary with Füger's. The portrait of Frau Henriette Pereira-Arnstein (Plate XXIV.) painted by him (or possibly after him) represents a lady who for many years played an important part in financial circles in Vienna. She was the daughter of Nathan Adam Arnstein, who was ennobled in 1795 and made a baron in 1798, and Fanny Itzig, daughter of Daniel Itzig, the Berlin banker. She was born in Berlin, and married Heinrich Pereira, whom her father had adopted, in Vienna in 1802. Wealthy, beautiful and witty, she entertained lavishly and, during the Vienna Congress, gathered diplomats of all countries to her salon. Her name is mentioned on nearly every page of the diaries of Friedrich von Gentz and the letters of Staegemann. Caroline Pichler mentions her with kindly warmth of feeling, for she was extremely charitable; she died in 1859 at the ripe age of seventy-nine in Vienna.

Two names stand high amongst the generation which followed Füger; Daffinger and Waldmüller.

Moritz Michael Daffinger (1790–1849), a native of Vienna, worked as a young man in the porcelain factory which was then at its zenith there. In 1809 he began to paint miniatures, and seized the opportunity of Thomas Lawrence's visit to Vienna in 1819 to study the technique of this most admired of portrait - painters. He became the painter of Viennese beauties, whose voluptuous charm had less of the ethereal and languishing element

No. 126. Denner. *Old Woman*

of the French and English women of that day. The painter was a handsome man but churlish, and does not seem to have been at all amiable in disposition. Costenoble, the actor, says of Daffinger in his diary: "The pleasures of this man consist of painting, quarrelling, being always in the right and never contented." He died of cholera. Grillparzer wrote his epitaph: "He sought Nature alone in the countenance of man and the world of flowers, but found her dressed in her bridal attire as Art." Just as Füger had painted the Society of the Austria of Joseph's day, so Daffinger painted the sunny side of the Austria of Metternich before the

Revolution of 1848. Those were the great days for Austria, when the Po was still an Austrian river and the politics of Europe had their origin at the Ballhausplatz in Vienna. The Duke of Reichstadt (p. 129) is the tragic figure of the period. While still in his cradle he was made King of Rome and called Majesty, and at three years of age received into his grandfather's guardianship—one might almost say imprisonment—and was not even vouchsafed a suitable title. In 1817 he was made Duke of Mödling, and a year later changed this title for the slightly less insignificant one of Duke of Reichstadt. From a Majesty the boy sank to a Highness, a petty revenge on a defenceless child worthy of Francis I. The young eagle pined in his cage. The descriptions of Prokesch-Osten, Lulu Thürheim and others who were allowed to approach him are more than touching, they are deeply affecting. The son of one of the greatest men known to history, who was born inheritor of an empire that included half Europe, ate out his heart in Austrian regimental service and died because he caught cold at the funeral parade of a mere subaltern. In Maria Theresa's palace at Schönbrunn, whence his father had dictated his laws to the conquered empire in 1809, he died in 1832 in the same room and on the same bed Napoleon had used.

Daffinger was closely in touch with the family of Prince Metternich and painted the greater, one may say the better, part of his portraits for the Princess's collection. He also painted her repeatedly. Countess Mélanie Zichy (p. 127) became Prince Metternich's third wife in 1831. He was fifty-eight years of age when he made this love-match. The marriage was a happy one. The young Princess was extremely temperamental, and was in the habit of speaking her mind. Once, when she met Louis Philippe's ambassador at a ball just after the Revolution of July, and he admired the tiara she was wearing, she replied: "Yes, it is beautiful, is it not, and it happens to have been honestly come by." The Frenchman complained to the Chancellor, but Metternich laughed, and said: "I married my wife, but I did not bring her up." Princess Mélanie was loyal to her husband and accompanied him on his dangerous flight from Vienna to London. Her diary is full of interesting notes on life in good Society at Vienna during "*Vormärz.*" The turban she wears in her portrait (Plate XXV.) was in fashion for ten years. It came from India to London and then became the fashion in Paris after the Egyptian Expedition, and remained in favour until the eighteen-forties. The Princess died in 1854, five years before her husband.

Countess Leontine Sandor (p. 127) was Prince Metternich's daughter by his first wife, Countess Eleonore Kaunitz. In 1835 she married the Hungarian Count Sandor, a famous sportsman, and became the mother of Princess Pauline, who married her mother's stepbrother, Richard Metternich, and thus completed the family circle. Count Sandor, through his reckless

No. 127. Runge. *Mother and Daughters*

daring, became crippled for life and his wife nursed and cared for him for many years. His daughter in her entertaining Reminiscences has related many of his mad pranks.

The Duchess von Sagan was Princess Katharine Friederike Wilhelmine Biron of Courland, who was born in 1781, married three times and divorced three times. She died in 1839. She was frequently seen in Society playing whist in company with her three divorced husbands—Prince Rohan, Prince Trubetzkoi and Count Schulenburg. She wished to be considered witty as well as beautiful. "She is always in breath-less haste to say nothing whatever," remarks Countess Lulu Thürheim of her.

Countess Crescenz Szechényi (p. 130) was the daughter of Count Karl August Seilern and Countess Maximiliane Wurmbrand. In 1819, at the age of twenty, she became the second wife of Count Karl Zichy, whose first wife was Countess Julie Festetics. The latter was much admired by Friedrich Wilhelm III. at the Vienna Congress on account of her resemblance to Queen Louise, and was known in Society as *"la beauté céleste."* Countess Crescenz married a second time in 1836, her husband being Count Stephan Szechényi, and died in 1875.

No. 128.   Stock.   *Frau von Stein*

Countess Sidonie Potocka (p. 126) was a grand-daughter of Prince de Ligne, famous for his wit. She married Count Franz Potocki in 1807 at the age of twenty-one and thereby became daughter-in-law to her own mother, for the latter, Hélène Apollonia, Princess Massalska, had married *en secondes noces* in 1794 Count Vincenz Potocki, the father of Count Franz. "We did not like Sidonie Ligne in spite of her wit," writes Lulu Thürheim, "for she had a mocking and spiteful tongue." The costume she wears in this portrait is characteristic of the fashion of the early 'thirties. There was a rage for ornaments, and people wore jewels on the forehead and a head-dress and sometimes a hat as well, on top of a mass of curls and puffs, and in addition as many feathers, ribbons, flowers, veils and brooches as there was room for! No doubt the fantastic turban of red and black striped silk with its mighty feathers suited the fair hair of the Countess.

Countess Sophie Narischkin (p. 133), painted by Daffinger in her childhood, married Count Schuwaloff. She was born in 1829 and died in 1894. Countess Nandine Karolyi (Plate XXVI.) was Countess Kaunitz-Rietberg and died in 1862, aged fifty-seven. Maria Felicitas Malibran (p. 134) was one of the most famous singers of the nineteenth century. She was the daughter of Manuel Garcia and became a *prima donna* at the age of seventeen. Possessing a soprano of unusual compass, she intoxicated the public whenever she was heard; she was the first singer to have her horses taken out and her carriage drawn home by gentlemen. She was divorced from her first husband and married the violinist de Bériot, but died in 1836 at the age of twenty-seven at Manchester, from overstrain. She was the successful rival of the opera-stars of her day, Henriette Sontag, Wilhelmine Schröder-Devrient, etc. In Paris she appeared at the same time as Devrient, and the two singers, for a jest, used to exchange rôles in *Othello*. Sometimes Malibran sang the part of Desdemona and Schröder-Devrient Othello; sometimes the dainty little Malibran was the Moor, and tall, stately Schröder-Devrient Desdemona.

Wilhelmine Schröder-Devrient (p. 135), daughter of the once famous tragedienne Sophie Schröder, must have had incomparable charm. Richard Wagner raves over the impression she made on him, for what her voice lacked in perfection she made up by passion and temperament; and not only on the stage. She was married three times—to Karl Devrient, the actor, to Baron von Döring, and lastly to Baron Bock, a Livonian. But her heart had room for more than these, and Karoline Bauer and other, possibly jealous, contemporaries cannot say enough about her adventures. She died in 1860, aged fifty-six.

Fanny Elssler (p. 135) was an artist to whom Nature had

No. 129.   Füger.   *Maria Theresa and her Family*

been prodigal of her gifts. She was dazzlingly beautiful and of great charm, and her powers of acting vied with her gift for dancing. "She dances history," they said in Berlin, and many years later Friedrich Pecht, Rudolf Delbrück and others who saw her wrote with enthusiasm of her in their Memoirs. She was graceful even in old age. For the times, the sums she earned were fabulous; she was paid 750,000 francs in America for playing in eight rôles. She died in 1884 in Vienna, her birthplace, at the age of seventy-four.

Though the art of the miniature depends more on beautifying the subject than is the case with high art, yet a true artist like Daffinger can choose the psychological moment for enshrining the characteristics of his sitter even in a small portrait. In the case of Franz Grillparzer (1791–1872) (p. 136) he has given an impression of that dissatisfaction and discontent which more and more darkened the poet's life. Chagrin over a failure made him sulk for years with the public, who paid no attention to the poet's ill-humour. It was said in Munich that he played the sulky child—and no one troubled about him! Not till his death did all his laboriously-concealed bitterness come to light, and when we hear of Kathi Fröhlich, the poet's "eternal love," we feel inclined to congratulate her because she was obliged to remain his "bride," and was not obliged to become his wife!

Adalbert Stifter's broad friendly face (p. 137) gives no hint either of the amiable poet or of the sufferer who was finally driven to commit suicide to put a voluntary end to unbearable pain. He was a school-inspector of Linz (1805–

No. 130. Füger. *Archduchess Marie Clementine*

1868), but his sympathetic descriptions of Nature, wherein he knew so well how to make wood and heath, mountain and plain re-echo his own mood, are not much read to-day.

Empress Marianne (Plate XXVII.) of Austria, whose portrait was painted by Emanuel Peter (1799–1873) from a sketch by Daffinger, was a pitiable sacrifice to State expediency. She was a daughter of King Victor Emanuel I. of Sardinia, and in 1831, at the age of twenty-eight, was married to Ferdinand, later Emperor of Austria. Imbecility is no bar to a throne, otherwise this unfortunate man (in South Germany

No. 131.   Füger.   *Archduke Joseph*

such folk are called "*Trottel*," or cretins), who could not have practised the humblest trade, would assuredly not have reigned. One could fill volumes with tales of the *bétises* he uttered, or which rumour has ascribed to him. The Empress passed her sorrowful and aimless life by his side and by this pitiable existence certainly earned beatification. She died in 1884. Archduchess Sophie (p. 139) was a daughter of King Max I. of Bavaria and sister of Queen Elizabeth of Prussia and of two Queens of Saxony. She married the Archduke Franz Karl at the age of nineteen, in 1824, and had many children. She was distinguished for her great energy and well knew how to

No. 132.   Füger.   *Archduchess Marie Christine and Duke Albert of Sachsen-Teschen*

Grassi. *Baroness Henrietta von Pereira-Arnstein*

Daffinger. *Princess Mélanie Metternich*

No. 133. Joseph Grassi.
Princess Josephine Auersberg and two children

make her influence operative. Politically she favoured the *ultra-montane* party, and is said to have made life by no means pleasant for her daughter-in-law, the Empress Elizabeth. She died in 1872, aged sixty-seven. Her son, the last Austrian Emperor, was painted, when Archduke, by Daffinger (p. 138), who has produced in this portrait a masterpiece of interpretation. He was called "the Emperor of Babel" in a French caricature, which certainly hit the nail on the head. How could that Babylonian confusion of tongues end otherwise than in catastrophe? Even such a strong and gifted personality as his could not hold such an Empire together. Franz Joseph was short-sighted enough to precipitate matters by his harsh treatment of the German element which was the chief support of his throne.

A rival for Society's favour was Ferdinand Georg Wald-müller (1793–1865), almost the same age as Daffinger and, like him, a 'Viennese. He was not, like Daffinger, exclusively a miniature-painter, but followed in Lawrence's footsteps, as Daffinger once had. He was one of those artists who see in academies both a danger and an advantage to art; in 1846 he wrote a pamphlet against academic instruction. His Family Portrait of an Unknown Lady and her Two Children (Plate XXVIII.) shows all the good points of his lovable and pleasing art; the three figures are characteristically conceived, well-arranged and the colours well-harmonised.

Besides Daffinger and Waldmüller there were numerous other miniaturists who have reached the same high level as these masters in at anyrate a few of their productions. There is the Court painter Bernhard von Guerard (d. 1836), for instance, and Kreizinger, who painted the Empress Marie Louise (p. 140). Marie Louise was just nineteen years of age when she was married to Napoleon. She was the daughter of the Emperor Francis I. of Austria, and grand-daughter of Queen Caroline of Naples, one of Napoleon's most bitter and irreconcilable enemies. She was devoid of grace, charm or taste. Amongst ladies who understood the art of dress, such as Caroline Pichler, there was only one opinion over the tasteless attire in which the young Archduchess was publicly seen. When at Braunau she put on the Parisian dresses brought by her new French suite, she looked a different woman, says Lulu Thürheim. Napoleon had her taught dancing in order that she might learn deportment and move gracefully. It is well known that she was not worthy of her great husband. She moped and was much piqued at the Vienna Congress because she was unable to join in the festivities. Napoleon was scarcely dead when she consoled herself with Count Adam Albrecht von Neipperg. When he died Count Charles René de Bombelles entered into the privilege of a morganatic husband. Marie Louise did not disdain the addresses of other young men besides. She managed her little dukedom of Parma well and died in 1847 on the eve of the Revolution.

Karl Agricola, of Säckingen in Baden, worked in Vienna from 1798 onwards. He received 100 ducats or more for his tasteful and careful little works. His portrait of his own family (Plate XXIX.) is considered by Franz Ritter his masterpiece. It was painted in 1815, and shows his mother, aged sixty-four, his wife Christine (*née* von Saar), and his boy. It shows taste, delicate feeling and loving care, and he received 300 guilders for it. He died in Vienna, which had become his home, in 1852.

The brilliance of the Viennese miniaturists has thrown the performances of many other German masters undeservedly into the shade, and we owe our knowledge of them to publications which have recently drawn our attention to their

No. 134. Füger. *Portrait of Man with Letter*

creations. For instance, the book on the miniature-collection of the Grand Duke of Hesse acquaints us with artists such as Friedrich Jakob Hill (1758–1846), who must henceforth be reckoned among the great miniature-painters. His self-portrait (Plate XXX.), which must have been painted in 1785, is a brilliant success. It is a masterpiece of characterisation, as distinguished for its sharpness of observation as for its delicate treatment of colour which, rigidly adhering to very few tones, produces a most striking effect. We ought certainly to accustom ourselves to the idea of mentioning this Court painter of Hessen-Darmstadt side by side with Füger, who had previously stood alone as a German miniaturist.

Miniature-painting was once, like painting on china, a favourite pursuit of dilettantism, for mere care, accuracy and taste were sufficient to produce quite respectable and pleasing results in the case of anyone with a moderate gift for drawing.

The fellow-countryman of Hill, Wilhelm von Harnier, counsellor to the Legation, though not on a par with Hill, produced in 1828 a very creditable piece of work with his portrait of Thérèse Pêche (Plate XXXI.). She was an ac-

No. 135.   Füger.   *Unknown Lady*

tress and, when young, so beautiful that she had to move from theatre to theatre in spite of her contracts, because the envy of her colleagues or the only too well-justified jealousy of Society women made it impossible for her to remain. She went from Hamburg to Darmstadt, then to Stuttgart, and finally to the Hofburg Theatre at Vienna. In Fröhlich's entertaining reminiscences, *Forty Years from the Life of a Corpse,* he states that Thérèse began her career as a snake-dancer in a travelling menagerie. As long as she was a young, beautiful and much-admired actress (the aged A. W. von Schlegel was "astonished, enchanted and amazed" by her) success was hers; but when she left tragic lover rôles and took up "catty" drawing-room parts, her acting became, as the malicious Moritz Gottlieb Saphir remarks, "the perfection of mediocrity." She married Herr Vimel de Jauzat in 1840 and died in 1882 at the age of seventy-two.

In the Scandinavian countries miniature-work was mostly carried on by foreigners —Dutch or English. But what artists like Alexander Cooper gave them was paid back in compound interest by such men as Boit, Lanfransen, Hall, Bruckmann and others.

Jacob van Dort was a foreigner who worked at a Scandinavian Court. He was a Dutchman, became Danish Court painter and lived at Copenhagen; he also worked at Stockholm. In Denmark he received twenty-five reichsthalers for each portrait. Queen Anna Katharina of Den-

No. 136. *Portrait of a Lady*

mark (Plate XXXII.) was a daughter of the Elector Joachim Friedrich of Brandenburg, and was married in 1597 at the age of twenty-two to King Christian IV., the Danish national hero. She was crowned in 1598 and died in 1612 at the palace in Copenhagen. Her son, who is represented beside her in this portrait, which was painted a year before her death, is Prince Christian, then eight years old. He was chosen heir to the throne by the Danish electors in 1608, but died a year before his father in 1647 at Schloss Körbitz, near Dresden. His brother, Frederick III., ascended the

Danish throne in his place and made it hereditary instead of elective.

Another Dutchman, Toussaint Gelton, became Court painter to Christian V. of Denmark. The aristocratic lady (Plate XXXIII.) with the King Charles spaniel and the love-birds is wearing a curious costume unlike the fashion of the seventeenth century. One of the earliest Danish miniature-painters is Adermann, an artist who seems to have lacked

No. 137. Daffinger. *Countess Sidonie Potocka*

originality. The portrait of Admiral Gyldenlöve (Plate XXXIV.) is at anyrate an exact copy of another miniature in which Hiller painted Prince Karl of Denmark after a portrait by Rigaud. Adermann has contented himself with altering the features slightly and filling the background with little ships. Ulrich Christian Gyldenlöve (1678–1719) was the son of King Christian V. and Sophie Amalie Moth and, on account of his exalted origin, adequately quali-fied for the post of High Admiral of Denmark.

Jorge Gylding was a painter of china and be-came Danish Court painter with an income of 300 reichsthalers per annum. He died in 1765. His con-nection with porcelain made it peculiarly suitable that he should paint the portrait of the monarch who possessed the most famous china factory in Europe — the Elector Friedrich August II. of

No. 138. Daffinger. *Princess Metternich*

Saxony, called King Augustus III. of Poland (Plate XXXV.). As a king without any power and obliged to support the chimera of a Polish crown with good Saxon thalers, he found Frederick the Great, as an opponent, too much for him. The thirty years, 1733–1763, during which he ruled Saxony, are the saddest in her history.

W. A. Müller, who worked at Copenhagen in the second half of the eighteenth century, painted a portrait of the painter Professor Pederals

No. 139. Daffinger. *Countess Sandor*

(Plate XXXVI.) and the sculptor Wiedewelt (Plate XXXVII.). Johann Wiedewelt, son and pupil of Just Wiedewelt, attended the *atelier* Coustous in Paris and went in the late autumn of 1754 to Rome to seek inspiration from the antique. There he became a friend of Winckelmann, with whom he lived in great intimacy for six months. He returned to Copenhagen, was made Director of the Academy of Art and was entrusted

by King Friederich V. with the duty of making the sculptures which adorn the Fredensborg Schlosspark.

For a long time he was the pride of his countrymen, but had the unhappy fate of living to see himself put utterly in the shade by Thorwaldsen. Finally, when ill and old and without means, he gave up the struggle and sought his own death on 21 December, 1802, in the Peblinger Lake.

C. Hoyer, a Danish miniaturist of the second half of the

No. 140.   Daffinger.   *Duchess of Sagan*

eighteenth century, painted the portrait of Queen Marie Sophie Friederike (Plate XXXVIII.). She was the daughter of the Landgrave Karl von Hesse and married in 1790, at the age of twenty-three, Prince Friedrich, who reigned from 1808 to 1839 as Friedrich VI. of Denmark. He was one of the monarchs present at the Vienna Congress in 1814, and his good-nature made him very generally popular there. He was less successful with his political aspirations, and when the Czar Alexander bade him farewell with the compliment,

"Your Majesty takes all our hearts with you," he replied with some wryness, "But not, I fear, your souls." The Queen lived until 1852.

Christian Hornemann (1765–1844), a native of Copenhagen, was educated in Germany, and from 1787 to 1803 lived some-times in Dresden and sometimes in Berlin. He painted Friedrich Wilhelm III. and Queen Louise. In 1804 he returned to Denmark and became Court painter. His self-portrait (Plate XXXIX.) must have been painted about the time of his return to Copenhagen. Christian VIII. (1786–1848. Plate XL.), son of the Crown Prince Friedrich and Princess Sophie Friederike of Mecklenburg-Schwerin, was chosen by the

No. 141.   Daffinger.   *Duke of Reichstadt*

Norwegians in 1813 for their king, a choice which was not ratified by the monarchs and diplomats of the Vienna Congress, who preferred to unite Norwegians and Swedes because they had less in common. He followed Friedrich VI. on the Danish throne in 1839 and reigned till 1848. In 1806 he had married Princess Charlotte of Mecklenburg-Schwerin, a marriage which was dissolved in 1809 when the Princess was surprised in an amour with a French musician, Edouard Dupuis. After this the temperamental lady lived in exile in Jutland, then she travelled about and finally died in 1840 at Rome in a convent. Now, after all her wanderings in the Wood of Error, she rests in the little German cemetery in the shade of St. Peter's, under the monument put up to her by her son.

No. 142. Daffinger.
Countess Crescenz Szechényi-Seilern

An industrious and original artist was the peasant's son, Hans Peter Feddersen of Schnatebüll, in the Tondern district (1788–1860). He used Chinese white on paper and his work was distinguished for its laborious accuracy and strong likeness. His gift never came to maturity. He only received one or two thalers for his portraits and, according to his own showing, painted about 6000 altogether. They are all done in profile. He painted the famous singer Angelica Catalani (p. 142) as she appeared on the concert platform. She was not only one of the most beautiful women of her time but a marvellous *bravura* singer. All Europe rang with her fame, for she travelled in every part. She detested Napoleon and kept out of his way, only coming to Paris after his downfall. In 1827 she closed her artistic career in Berlin, but did not die till 1849, in Paris, of cholera. She is buried in the Campo Santo at Pisa.

THE MINIATURE AND ITS
APPLICATION

THE MINIATURE AND ITS APPLICATION

Jewellery, Fans, etc.

In earlier times the uses to which the miniature was put were very varied. To-day a small portrait or photograph is only used as the embellishment—or the reverse—of a drawing-room and but very seldom met with in the form of jewellery; even then it usually only appears as a brooch or pendant and not amongst the better classes. In the past, however, the miniature was met with everywhere in the form of jewellery or ornamental household effects.

At the beginning of the sixteenth century gentlemen wore costly jewels on their headgear. In the Imperial Hofmuseum at Vienna there are golden medallions for hats, of Spanish workmanship of the year 1520, with miniature-portraits in enamel of the Emperor Charles V. Even before the introduction of miniature-painting it was the custom for princes to bestow, as reward for some special service, a gold chain and portrait of themselves. The chains of office of mayors and other

No. 143.   Daffinger.
Countess Sophie Schuwaloff, née Narischkin

city worthies survive as a remembrance of this custom. This type of gift, which one so often sees depicted in old portraits, had the advantage over the Orders of the present day that it was regarded at the same time as an honour and a monetary recompense. The portraits were nearly always golden medals or coins, and not till the sixteenth century were they replaced by miniature-paintings.

No. 144.   Daffinger.
The Prima-donna Malibran-Garcia

In 1558 Sir Francis Walsingham received a valuable jewel from Queen Elizabeth after the defeat of the Armada. It still exists and is a gold medal with a portrait of the Queen in relief on the obverse, and on the reverse a representation in enamel of the dispersal of the Spanish fleet; within is a miniature-portrait in gouache of the Queen by Nicholas Hilliard. James I. honoured Thomas Lyte of Lytes Cary, in Somerset, who had prepared the King's genealogical tree, with a similar costly gift that is now in Lord Rothschild's Waddesdon bequest at the British Museum. It consists of an enamelled medallion set with pearls and precious stones, whose exquisite workmanship Williamson ascribes to the famous jeweller Daniel Mignot. It contains a miniature of James I. painted by Isaac Oliver. Queen Christina of Sweden, Gustavus Adolphus's eccentric daughter, presented to General Niclaes Desmel in 1650 a gold chain worth 284 thalers with her portrait,

Daffinger. *Countess Karolyi-Kaunitz in Riding Habit*

Peter (after Daffinger). *The Empress Marianne of Austria*

for which Alexander Cooper had been paid nine ducats. When dismissing the French Ambassador she presented him with a gold chain worth 198 crowns and a portrait - medallion worth 390 thalers. Long after the conferring of Orders had become the custom, reigning princes clung to the habit of giving their portrait to those they wished to honour. King Stanislaus August Poniatowski presented his motherly friend Madame Geoffrin with his portrait set with brilliants on her departure from

No. 145.   Daffinger.
Wilhelmine Schröder-Devrient

Warsaw on the 10th September, 1766. She kept the portrait but returned the diamonds.

Frederick the Great used to pay ruinous sums for presents of this kind; Ephraim and Sons delivered him in 1745 at Breslau a portrait set with brilliants for 4400 thalers, and in 1763 the same firm received 3000 thalers for a similar order. Witwe Reclam and Son received 3600 thalers in 1764 for a portrait of the King in a frame and crown of diamonds. Field-

No. 146.   Daffinger.   *Fanny Elssler*

No. 147.   Daffinger.   *Franz Grillparzer*

Marshal Lehwald, in a portrait of himself hanging in the palace at Berlin, is seen to be wearing a miniature of Frederick the Great (p. 146), framed in diamonds, that is possibly by Chodowiecki; in the Hohenzollern Museum is a portrait of Countess Voss, Queen Louise of Prussia's lady-in-waiting, and it can be seen that she is wearing round her neck, on the orange ribbon of the Order of the Black Eagle, a portrait of Friedrich Wilhelm III. framed in diamonds. Marshal Berthier was given a miniature-portrait of the Emperor Francis II. in Vienna in 1810 with the Order of the Golden Fleece which, including the brilliants, had cost 150,000 francs and was certainly worth 96,000 francs. Napoleon, in return, gave Count Metternich, the Austrian ambassador, his portrait in a medallion, which was worth 150,000 francs.

This list could be considerably extended, especially if one includes Russian dignitaries of the late eighteenth and early nineteenth centuries. Count de la Garde saw Countess Protassoff at the Vienna Congress bedecked with diamond-studded

No. 148.   Daffinger.   *Adalbert Stifter*

portraits of the young men whose suitability it had been her duty to test for the Empress Catherine II. Catherine had sent Gregor Orlow her portrait in a heart-shaped medallion, with permission to wear it in his buttonhole; when Wassilschikoff superseded him in her favour, she demanded the return of this love-token; Orlow sent her the medallion and diamonds but kept the portrait. Catherine's ladies-in-waiting wore a miniature of their royal mistress as a sign of office. The Sultan of Zanzibar presented the Emperor William I. with his portrait framed in brilliants on a broad moiré-ribbon instead of an Order.

The medallion miniature-portrait was to be found as a piece of jewellery pure and simple as early as the sixteenth century. The Jeffery Whitehead Collection contains a portrait of Mary Queen of Scots by Nicholas Hilliard set in diamonds and made still more precious because it contains a lock of the hair of that unhappy Queen. A portrait of her son James I., likewise by Nicholas Hilliard and still in its original setting of

K

brilliants, reached the figure of £2855 at the auction of the Duke of Hamilton's collection.

On the occasion of Charles IX.'s betrothal to the Archduchess Elizabeth in 1570 the bridegroom presented the bride's family with a splendid jewel, which is still to be seen in the Hofmuseum at Vienna (p. 143). It is an oval medallion of gold on the front of which Fides and Justitia are holding a wreath over a crown resting on two pillars. On the other side two intertwined C's are surmounted by a crown and surrounded by a wreath of flowers. Inside are miniature-portraits on vellum of Charles IX. of France and his mother, Catherine de Médicis, of Clouet's school.

No. 149.   Daffinger.
Franz Joseph, Emperor of Austria

Schloss Rosenborg in Copenhagen is particularly rich in miniature-portraits of the period of Alexander Cooper; many are in gold medallions decorated in enamel with monograms, symbols and all the favourite conceits of that age.

Peter Adolph Hall painted a portrait of the Dauphin for his betrothed, Marie Antoinette. He received 2664 francs for his work and the diamond setting cost 78,678 francs in addition; M. V. Costa painted a miniature of the Queen wearing this ornament on her corsage.

We have already mentioned the 175,000 franc medallion sent by Napoleon to his betrothed. When Marie Louise bade farewell to her Austrian suite at Braunau on 16 March, 1810, she presented, amongst other mementoes, three medallions containing a portrait of her consort, each worth from 7000 to 8000 francs. The imperial pair stood sponsor to twenty-five infants at Fontainebleau in November 1810. Each infant received as christening gift a medallion with miniature portraits of its exalted godparents and their monogram in diamonds; the twenty-five medallions cost, in all, 135,000 francs.

During the Empire it was the fashion to wear whole necklaces of miniatures strung together. Isabey painted a set of octagonal portraits for a necklace for Caroline Murat, Queen of Naples, and a similar row of portraits of the imperial family for a necklace for the Empress Marie Louise. Another of her necklaces has miniatures of all the Austrian archduchesses.

Philippe Soiron of Geneva, who worked in

No. 150.   Daffinger.   *Archduchess Sophie*

Paris at this time, made up a necklace of this kind for the Duchess of Montebello. Its central ornament was five miniatures in enamel of the Duchess's children, all with angels' wings, in the sweet and affected style introduced by Andrew Plimer when he painted his daughter Selina as a cherub. Marie Louise had the King of Rome painted in this style and gave the miniature, in the form of a bracelet, to her sister. Friedrich Johann Gottlieb Lieder painted Eugène Beauharnais' five children at Vienna in 1815, all as angels with coloured

No. 151. Kreizinger.   *Empress Marie Louise*

wings. At the exhibition of miniatures held at Mannheim in 1909 there was shown a bracelet, brooch and earrings made up of portraits in enamel; it was the wedding present in 1813 of Frau von Renz, *née* von Stockhausen.

There is another side to the history of the medallion-miniature. Madame de Motteville tells in her Memoirs how a miniature of the Duchess of Orleans that the enamoured Count Guiche was wearing round his neck saved his life in a battle, for a shot flattened itself against the portrait. Goethe, in *Wilhelm Meister*, makes his hero put the beloved Countess in danger of death by embracing her so passionately that she is seriously hurt by the miniature of her husband which she is wearing on her breast.

Miniatures were much used as bracelets, and in the sixteenth

Waldmüller. *Family Group*

Agricola. *Mother and Wife of the Artist*

and first half of the seventeenth centuries were also worn by
men, not only by young exquisites, but also dignified and
elderly men, such as the famous Sully for instance, who was
very proud of his.

Alexander Cooper was paid forty thalers apiece for the
bracelet-miniatures he painted at the Swedish Court in 1653.
Later, when the art of diamond-cutting was understood,
bracelets became more expensive. The Count of Provence,
when Louis XVIII., had himself painted by Hall, and the
miniature set as a bracelet with sixteen diamonds, which
cost him 15,552 francs. The fashion was also popular in circles
which had to be content with a less expensive form of jewellery.
In 1779 travellers to Paris noticed that even the market
women selling butter and eggs wore portraits of their lovers
on bracelets. One of the last commissions under the old régime
was Count Montmorin's order on 18 March, 1789, to the
jeweller Solle for two bracelets with miniatures of the King
and Queen set in diamonds, for 9000 francs each. They were
for a present, perhaps the last in the old munificent style.

The age of sentimentality brought in ornaments made of
hair. What a sweet indulgence it was to wear the hair of the
loved one as an ornament, and thereby to feel one's self so
closely in sympathy! Even Napoleon fell a victim to this
fashion and, at St. Helena, wore a watch-chain made out of
Marie Louise's hair. At the Mannheim Exhibition there was
shown a bracelet made of plaited hair and having a miniature
framed in gold of Countess Caroline Ysenburg, *née* Countess
Bentheim. Miniatures in diamond clasps on bracelets of real
pearls remained longest in favour, and we can remember
many such youthful portraits of the Empress Elizabeth of
Austria and other great ladies. There are some beautiful
pieces of jewellery in the miniature-collection of the Grand
Duke of Hesse. A bracelet of gold (p. 149) and Indian diamonds
contains a portrait of Prince Albert painted in enamel by
Henry Bone. The young Queen Victoria had to decide between
the Coburg-Gotha brothers, Albert and Ernest (later " Schützen-
Ernst "), and chose the handsomer. His was an exalted lot, but

was it a happy one? Parliament was niggardly with money, the Government provided no particular position for him, the nobility treated him with deliberate discourtesy, and the press followed suit. Everything he did was jeered at by *Punch*; his German accent, his clothes and manners were all laughed at. He bore himself with tact and intelligence in his difficult position and was as successful as circumstances allowed. The Great Exhibition in London was his idea and also South Kensington Museum. He died in 1861, but not until after his death were his services to the country recognised.

No. 152. H. P. Feddersen.
Angelica Catalani

The art of the miniature encourages the production of small works of handicraft. Lemberger mentions Niclas Prugger, who painted seven portraits of the Bavarian Electress Maria Anna on plates of copper the size of a groschen. It was not long before people began to wear miniatures in rings. The Hofmuseum at Vienna has some very interesting rings left by the Habsburg emperors. There is a lady's ring of gold and enamel (p. 150) with a revolving centrepiece showing the arms of Austria and Burgundy, and containing minute portraits of Emperor Matthias (1557–1619) and his consort the Empress Anna (1585–1618). The work was probably done on the occasion of their betrothal in 1611. Another ring is of gold and enamel and shows a portrait of the Empress Claudia Felicitas (1653–1676) under crystal. King Charles I. of England had a ring with a medallion containing his portrait and on the outside a death's head and the monogram C.R. in enamel; he gave it to Colonel Yates shortly before his death. This interesting treasure was sold at auction in London in 1877 and only fetched sixty-three pounds. Charles presented Sir Edmund Verney, one of his officers, with another ring containing his portrait, several years before his death; the miniature on this ring was not enclosed, but was protected under crystal. The miniatures in rings ought really all to be under tabular cut diamonds. Considering the limited space at the artist's disposal in the case of ring-miniatures one would

No. 153.   *Medallion of Gold and Enamel containing the Miniatures by Clouet. See p. 47*

expect it to be difficult, if not impossible, to produce a satisfactory effect. But it was not so. Carlo Gonzaga, Duke of Mantua, caught sight of a lady's portrait in a ring worn by the Duke of Lesdiguières in 1703 and fell deeply in love. Unfortunately she happened to be the Duchess and he had to bridle his passion. Scarcely was the Duke dead, however, when Gonzaga travelled to France to cast himself at his beloved's feet. She was quite unmoved by this devotion, would not even see Gonzaga, and even the authority of Louis XIV. did not avail to make the stubborn beauty change her mind.

In 1749 the Duchesse de Brissac received a ring with a movable bezel, on each side of which was a portrait of one of the King's daughters painted by Drouais and set by Leguay.

Cazaubon in 1762 painted portraits of Madame Adelaide de France with her sisters Madame Sophie and Madame Louise, for a ring. For this laborious work he received 1500 francs.

In 1773 Marie Antoinette, in a letter to her mother, said she was wearing portraits of her brothers in a ring. When Prince Henry of Prussia was in St. Petersburg in 1771, Queen Catherine presented him with her portrait in a ring set with diamonds.

In 1777 Mr. Craufurt gave the Marquise du Deffand a ring containing Voltaire's portrait.

The Blarenberghe family were very famous for their minute paintings. One of them painted a view of Château Menars for a ring for the Marquis de Menars; Noël painted four marine subjects in the four seasons; all four were enclosed in the bezel of a ring which could be opened and shut.

Engravers vied with miniaturists. Noël le Mire made a double portrait of Louis XV. and Henry IV. in so small a compass that it could be set in a ring. The Baronne du Montet saw in the possession of the Marquise de Laage an artificial rose that Marie Antoinette had once given to the Princesse de Lamballe; it had a portrait of the Queen hidden amongst its petals.

No. 154. *Pendant with Miniature of Louis XV. when a Child, framed in Diamonds*

In 1765 Chodowiecki received 411 thalers for twenty miniature-portraits of Prince Henry of Prussia, which took him four months to paint and were intended for rings and lockets. There were four portrait-rings of this kind amongst the effects of Frederick the Great. He was fond of giving presents and he paid the well-known Gotzkowski in 1743, 1300 thalers for a ring with his portrait; in 1746, 950 thalers for two rings with portraits, and 550 thalers to Ephraim and Sons in 1744 for a diamond portrait-ring.

About 1770 it became the fashion in Paris for gentlemen to wear large buttons on their coats, and as these buttons rapidly grew larger and larger, the idea of painting on them developed. Bachaumont writes in his private Memoirs, 18 November, 1786:

There is no fashion which the folly, superficiality and passion for excess of our *élégants* does not reduce to a foolish idiosyncrasy. They have driven this craze for buttons to ridiculous lengths and now wear them not only of inordinate size—as big as a six-franc piece —but with miniatures or whole pictures on them, so that some sets cost fabulous sums. One man will have a set of buttons depicting the first twelve Roman emperors, another reproductions of antique statues or Ovid's *Metamorphoses*. At the Palais Royal there was one shameless fellow who had Aretino's postures on his buttons, so that respectable ladies, on drawing near him, did not know which way to look.

Fragonard painted a set of buttons with scenes from Watteau; a young lady presented her bridegroom with a set reproducing the best-known paintings of Greuze. Many of the most famous miniaturists began their career in this way, and it is known that Hall, the Blarenberghes and Dumont painted on buttons. Dumont received two to three francs a button, but some sets of a dozen cost a thousand francs or more. Isabey began his career in this way, and himself relates how he decorated buttons with cupids, flowers, landscapes, etc., for which he was paid twelve sols apiece. Love scenes and landscapes were followed by flower pieces, imitation cameos, emblems, insects and heaven knows what beside. By 1788 fashion had aspired to architectural subjects and bore representations of some of France's most famous buildings on its buttons.

During the Revolution, patriotic buttons replaced all others, and representations of the taking of the Bastille, heads of Necker, Marat, Lepelletier de St. Fargeau and other notabilities took the place of more fanciful subjects. Lamartine maintains that buttons were even decorated with pictures of the guillotine, but Maze-Sencier has proved that the poet invented this.

The fashion was amusing enough to be imitated in Germany. Baron Schilling von Cannstatt of Stuttgart possesses a set of twenty-two ivory buttons painted with representations of the palace and grounds of the Ludwigsburg at Saarbrücken. The art dealer Hieronymus Löschenkohl had buttons manufactured to order in Vienna from 1787 onwards with miniatures behind glass. For instance, one could have a set illustrating the *Sorrows of Werther*; on ivory and set with precious stones they cost from four florins to twelve ducats; cheaper ones were "made of straw in the latest fashion."

We must likewise include rosaries where the Cross, of silver filigree perhaps, had the Crucifixion painted in enamel. The Imperial Schatzkammer (Treasure-house) in Vienna possesses a seventeenth-century rosary with ten beads of crystal, each of which contains pictures of the saints or scenes from the Passion in "Pallion" painting.

No. 155. *The Lehwald jewelled Miniature of Frederick the Great*

The miniature appeared mostly in conjunction with boxes of various kinds. In the sixteenth century and later people had flat boxes of wood or metal to protect the great hanging seals they attached to deeds and documents. These boxes were used also to keep miniatures in, and there are portraits of Henry VIII., ascribed to Holbein, in ivory boxes bearing the Tudor rose on the back and front. Sometimes miniatures are met with in hollowed-out coins.

After the middle of the seventeenth century the snuff-box came into general favour. Royal persons presented ambassadors, diplomats and Court servants with gold boxes containing their portrait. It was a tactful form of money present, and its value varied according to the importance of the receiver—it might be necessary to honour him or to put him under an obligation. King Charles Gustavus X., who followed Christina on the Swedish throne, had three gold boxes made, studded with diamonds and painted with his miniature by Alexander Cooper, in 1656. One, worth 500 thalers, was for General Fleetwood; another, worth 700 thalers, for Gustav Bielke, the Swedish ambassador to Russia, and the third, which cost 3600 thalers, went to the Danish ambassador, General Willem Drakenshelm. In ever-practical England the bearer of such costly gifts expected a present for himself, and in 1699 the Saxon envoy von Bose received his portrait snuff-box only after he had paid a *douceur* of sixty pounds. The royal gift of a snuff-box and portrait became almost a national institution under Louis XIV. Maze-Sencier, in the interest of collectors, has searched French archives and brought together in his industrious compilations a great mass of dates, figures and information of all kinds. The Louis Quatorze snuff-boxes were not really *tabatières*, for they bore the King's portrait on the inside of the lid and were only regarded as a means of enshrining it; the amount of gold and the precious stones represented the amount of money the king wished to give. The French themselves reaped the least advantage from these presents; whilst no Frenchman received a box worth more than 2400 francs, foreign diplomats repeatedly obtained boxes worth a small fortune. In 1668 Prince Dietrichstein, the imperial ambassador, received a snuff-box worth 8440 francs, the Duke of Buckingham one worth 28,000 francs, the Duchess of York, wife of the Duke of York (later James II.), one worth

33,000 francs in 1673, and during the years when Louis XIV. thought to draw England over to his side, the English were singled out for preference. In the accounts we find in 1678 the English ambassador receiving a box worth 11,315 francs; in 1679 the Earl of Sunderland one worth 14,183 francs; in the same year the Earl of Oxford one of 12,288 francs; 1690, Lord

No. 156. Unknown.
Pendant Miniature of the Emperor Joseph II.

Tyrconnel received a snuff-box with a portrait and forty-eight brilliants worth 21,218 francs. At the same time the envoys of less important countries received much more modest gifts. Herr von Bernstorff, the Danish ambassador, received a portrait snuff-box in 1683 worth 4628 francs; Baron von Schönborn, the ambassador from Kurmainz, had one in 1698 worth 6436 francs; Baron von Schulenburg, the minister from Braunschweig-Wolfenbüttel, one worth 4218 francs; Count Sinzendorf, the imperial ambassador, of whom Liselotte has given such a bad account, had to be satisfied with a box worth 4860 francs in 1701, whilst Cardinal Ottoboni in 1703 received a snuff-box set with diamonds and worth 24,677 francs. The miniature-portraits on these boxes are in enamel or gouache and are by Bruckmann, Perrault, Petitot, Chatillon and Ferrand, and the goldsmith's work was done by Pitan until 1676, and after that until the King's death by Pierre le Tessier de Montarsy.

Louis XIV. abhorred tobacco and, though smoking was out of the question amongst the better classes, snuff-taking was a very general habit and had even established itself at Versailles in spite of the openly-expressed disapproval of the King. The Duchess of Orleans wrote of this habit that it was disgusting to see the ladies with their noses all dirty from the snuff and reeking of it. After the death of the *roi soleil* the snuff-box with the portrait on the inside of its lid gave way to the true snuff-box with the portrait on the outside. Its use as a present remained the same and its value varied likewise in accordance with the importance of the person to whom it was presented. In 1719 the Regent sent a beautiful snuff-box with a portrait and fifty-three brilliants worth, in all, 31,000 francs to the Abbé Dubois as a present for a mysterious unknown L. C. A. In 1720 the register of the King's gifts

No. 157. *Bracelet containing Miniature Portrait of Prince Albert*

mentions a fabulously valuable *tabatière* that Marquis Scotti, the envoy from Parma, received, with a portrait of the young King painted by Massé in a setting of forty-two brilliants and fifteen rose-diamonds, worth 129,852 francs. "You will never see its like," says Maze-Sencier.

The Regent was by no means stingy with official presents. In 1720 he gave Lord Stair, the English ambassador, a snuff-box worth 49,805 francs, with a miniature of Louis XV. by Massé in a circle of fifty-three diamonds. When the Duchess of Montellano accompanied the Spanish Infanta Maria Anna Viktoria to Paris in 1721 (where the little princess was to be brought up until her marriage with the young King), she received a box set with diamonds worth 35,225 francs. A few years afterwards the Infanta was sent home again and Louis XV. married Maria Lesczynska.

Under Louis XV. the value of the *tabatière* with the royal portrait declined somewhat; the civilians came off worst. The ambassador from the Palatinate, Sibenius, received one in 1742 worth only 1800 francs, whilst the Danish ambassador,

Baron Vrindt, was given one worth 5078 francs in the same year. In 1747 von Schwerin, Frederick the Great's Master of the Horse, received a snuff-box worth 6709 francs, and the Württemberg ambassador, Baron von Keller, just such another. The *tabatières* given to Baron von Wrede in 1753, Count Reventlow in 1757, Prince Galitzin in 1758, and Count Dietrichstein in 1763, were worth from 6000 to 8000 francs.

In 1757 Maria Theresa sent Prince Lobkowitz to the French Court to announce the victory of the Austrians over the Prussians at Breslau, and he was rewarded with a snuff-box which had cost 18,317 francs; the miniature was by Le Brun

No. 158. *Ring with movable Bezel and Portrait of the Archduke Matthias*, 1611

No. 159. *The same Ring showing Portrait of the Archduchess Anna*

and the jewellery by Ducrollay. On exceptional occasions the value of these boxes exceeded the average, which was usually round about 10,000 francs. Count Tschernitscheff, the Russian ambassador, was given one worth 13,526 francs in 1762; in 1768 the Marquis de Mello one worth 26,578 francs. The Duke of Bedford's was worth 34,289 francs, and Count Viri, ambassador from Sardinia, received one worth 56,258 francs.

In 1752 a strange thing happened; some *tabatières* must have been returned by those for whom they were intended. The Mayor of Zurich, Herr Friesen, and Füssli the Stadtholder of the Zurich canton, who had organised a regiment of Swiss for French service, were each to be given snuff-boxes worth 2000 francs; they never accepted them, though the reason is not known.

It need hardly be explained that valuable snuff-boxes such as these were not intended for use, they merely represented a money gift that delicacy could not permit in a cruder form. That this was understood is proved by various occurrences. In 1755 Count Bellegarde, Minister Plenipotentiary of the King of Poland, received a snuff-box with a portrait worth 8000 francs; after his death his daughter sent it back and received the money in exchange. In 1770 the Danish ambassador, Baron Gleichen, was to receive a *tabatière*, but preferred to take the 15,000 francs in cash, though he begged, as a polished courtier, to be allowed only to keep the king's portrait, a miniature by Welper. In the same year the Nuncio preferred a present of 16,000 francs to a *tabatière*, and both these boxes were given to Walpole, the English ambassador.

A curious thing happened to Count Viri, the Sardinian ambassador. He received, on the occasion of the marriage of Madame Clothilde de France with the Prince of Piedmont in 1775, a snuff-box which had cost 29,940 francs. He sold it back to the jeweller Solle for 25,500 francs and, two years later, when he was recalled, received the same box again as a present! He sold it a second time, and finally it was given to Marquis Caraccioli, the King of Naples' ambassador, in 1781.

The artists most often employed by Louis XV. for the portraits on these boxes were Massé, Le Brun, Vincent, Penel, Charlier, Cazaubon, etc., and the enamel-workers Liotard, Rouquet, Durand and Bourgoing. The jewellery was by Solle, Jacqmin, Demay, Rondé and other goldsmiths.

During the reign of Louis XVI. *tabatières* began to be very richly set with diamonds. Prince Pamphili, the Nuncio who came to Paris in 1782 for the christening of the Dauphin, was given a snuff-box with a portrait of the King by Siccardi set with 173 diamonds and worth 29,000 francs. Fitzherbert, the English ambassador, received one in 1783 with 240 brilliants worth 21,585 francs, and in the same year the Duke of Manchester had one with 325 diamonds worth 31,453 francs.

The presents to the ambassadors of the small German states were much more modest. Count Loos, ambassador of the Saxon Electorate, was given a box worth 12,340 francs. The imperial ambassador Count Mercy-Argenteau received one

No. 160. *Gold Tabatière with Portraits of Maria Theresa and her Family*

worth 9632 francs in 1780. In 1785 Baron Schönfeld, the Saxon ambassador, received a snuff-box with 456 diamonds worth 17,510 francs. One of the least valuable *tabatières* went to the Canon Guaita, who brought a relic from the Cathedral Chapter of Aachen to the Queen, which was supposed to help to a fortunate issue in her confinement. He received a snuff-box with fifty brilliants and the King's portrait by Pasquier, worth 3440 francs.

It was also customary in Louis XVI.'s reign to return these costly presents. Prince Bariatinski, Catherine II.'s ambassador, immediately returned the *tabatière* he received in 1783 and which had cost 24,816 francs, and was paid 24,360 francs instead. He did the same two years later, when he was given, as a parting gift, a *tabatière* with 428 brilliants. This time he kept the King's portrait and yet obtained 24,000

Friedr. Joh. Hill. *Self Portrait*

Harnier.   *Thérèse Peche*

No. 161. *Gold Tabatière with portraits of Maria Theresa and her Family*

francs in cash for the rest, though the whole thing had cost 24,140 francs.

There is an interesting *tabatière* which was given to Benjamin Franklin, United States ambassador, on 7 June, 1785. It contained a portrait of the King by Siccardi, beset with 421 brilliants and valued at 16,103 francs. The artists who painted for Louis XVI. were usually I. D. Welper and Siccardi; the goldsmith's work was nearly always by Solle.

The general use of snuff by all—men and women and even children—led to great elaboration in the boxes which contained the precious luxury. According to Madame de Genlis, the first to use a box of old Chinese lacquer for snuff was Louvois, the War Minister. Monsieur de la Popelinière is supposed to have been the first to change the boxes into genuine tobacco-boxes by having the portrait on the outside of the lid. The *tabatière*

L

No. 162.   *Lid of Snuff-box, showing 28 Portraits of Members of Frederick the Great's Family*

quickly became an object of luxury and extravagance in the eighteenth century, and Mercier says that a Parisian gentleman of fashion needed a different one almost every day. No sooner were they made of the rarest and most costly materials—gold, silver, ivory, mother-of-pearl, semi-precious stones, marble, porcelain, lacquer—than the passion of the collector fell upon these charming objects. Prince Conti is said to have possessed 800 *tabatières*; the Saxon minister, Count Brühl, had hundreds, for he used a different one every day just as he put on a different dress or stock. "There is nothing finer than this collection," wrote Count Lehndorff in his diary in 1756, after he had looked at Brühl's collection of *tabatières*. Prince Conti, who died in 1776, left 800 snuff-boxes; the Pompadour ninety-eight alone of solid gold. The Duchess of Portland had hundreds of boxes left by her mother, the Countess of Oxford, and Horace Walpole writes to Mann of Lady Mary Wortley Montagu's son in 1751: "He possesses more snuff-boxes than a Chinese idol with a hundred noses could possibly use." This indulgence was almost the only one Frederick the Great allowed himself. He limited the household allowance to 22,000 thalers, a bagatelle when one remembers the sums swallowed up by his contemporary sovereigns for Court expenses, and only gave large sums for *tabatières*, his one luxury. Thiébault says in his *Reminiscences of Twenty Years at the Berlin Court*, writing of Frederick the Great: "I have only known him to have one luxury—the snuff-box. He possessed, they say, 1500 of these boxes, some of great beauty. He only took Spanish snuff." Nicolai, a contemporary of Frederick, reckoned the number of his snuff-boxes at 300 only and valued them altogether at 1,750,000 thalers, single ones having frequently cost between 2000 and 10,000 thalers. Amongst the King's effects after his death were found 120 snuff-boxes set with diamonds, and seven of these, each valued at 10,000 thalers, had been left by Frederick in his will to various persons. The King had a particular liking for Silesian chrysoprase, an opaque stone of dirty green colour which he had made into *tabatières* richly set with diamonds. He also possessed numerous snuff-boxes with portraits, one of amber and a portrait surrounded with diamonds, another of tortoiseshell with two portraits. The Hohenzollern Museum possesses a snuff-box with twenty-eight miniatures in four rows on the cover representing members of Frederick the Great's family (p. 154). In addition to collecting these boxes himself Frederick also gave them with his own portrait as presents. In 1746 Gotzkowski supplied him with a golden *tabatière* and portrait set with diamonds for 600 thalers; in 1748 one for 430 thalers; in 1751 a simpler one for 120 thalers. In 1753, on the occasion of a visit from the Court of Ansbach to Berlin, the Lady of the Bedchamber was given a portrait *tabatière* worth 280 thalers. In 1762 the Jordan brothers supplied a golden snuff-box with portrait set in brilliants for 6500 thalers.

Seidel, who gathered all these facts together from documents of the royal household, could not, however, inform us for whom this costly present was intended. When the King's funds were low he would give snuff-boxes somewhat poor in gold and without stones, sweetening the gift with the observation, "Friendship makes the gift more precious." When the Abbé Giustiniani celebrated him in an ode, doubtless in hopes of a princely reward, Frederick sent him a horn snuff-box, assuming that his vow of poverty would not permit him to accept gold!

No. 163. *Lacquer Box with Portrait of the "Great Landgravine"*

The rage for *tabatières* was not confined to France alone. Maria Theresa presented her brother-in-law, the Duke Charles of Lorraine, in 1764, with a magnificent *tabatière* of gold with green transparent enamel (pp. 152, 153). On the lid were the monograms of Maria Theresa and the Emperor Francis in diamonds, with portraits of the Archdukes Leopold and Joseph on either side, underneath portraits of the Empress in widow's weeds, and all round eight miniatures of the rest of her children. The painting was by Antonio Pencini or Bencini, who studied in Vienna in 1741 and became Court painter in 1753. The goldsmith's work was by Franz von Mackh. After the Duke's death Prince Kaunitz received the box and it is in the Vienna Hofmuseum to-day.

The Empress Elizabeth of Russia honoured the Marquis de la Chétardie, who helped her to gain the throne, with a snuff-box worth 50,000 roubles containing her portrait framed in diamonds. When Gustavus III. of Sweden visited Catherine II. at St. Petersburg in 1777 and was about to take his departure in the July of that year, each monarch presented the other's suite with the most exquisite and costly portrait *tabatières*; Melchior Grimm, in his correspondence, is never tired of praising them. Catherine admired Voltaire very greatly, and, wishing to show him especial honour, sent Prince Koslowski in 1769 to Ferney to present the author with an ivory snuff-box which she had made herself. It had her portrait framed in diamonds on the lid.

The custom of giving these *tabatières* for presents became such an understood thing at Court that we find Marshal Castellane, who was sent by Napoleon in 1809 to his brother, complaining bitterly in his diary that both King Jerome at Cassel and King Louis at the Hague let him depart without giving him a snuff-box.

As a valued article of luxury and fashion the snuff-box also played an important part in adventures of gallantry or the intimacies of daily life. Monsieur Dupin de Francueil, George Sand's grandfather, who was a very gay dog, had a *tabatière* made for Madame d'Epinay on which he himself was represented lying at her feet in a scene they had acted in amateur theatricals. She writes in her reminiscences, "The attitude and expression were so passionate and true."

The Marquise de Pompadour gave Comte Saint-Germain a snuff-box with a miniature of one of the seven sages of Greece, intended as a compliment to the recipient. The Marquise du Deffand gave a surprise present to Horace Walpole, who was devoted to the Marquise de Sévigné, consisting of a snuff-box containing the portrait of this charming woman and her monogram in marcasite. She also gave him a box with a miniature of her lap-dog on it, and to the Duchesse de Choiseul one on which her own hair was twisted to represent a piece of moss-agate.

The artist Johann Georg Wille gave 476 livres in 1765 for a gold *tabatière* for his wife, though he certainly gave twice as much for his own. The good man speaks in his diary very

No. 164. *Letter Case of Red Morocco with Portrait of Queen
Marie Lesczynska*

feelingly of his son, who gave him a box of red lacquer in
May 1769, on the lid of which he had painted a little Society
scene. The flattered parent adds that the box had cost the boy
12 louis d'or.

When the Maréchale de Luxembourg visited the Duc de
Choiseul in exile at Chanteloup in November 1771, she took
with her two snuff-boxes with his portrait on them. The most
splendid one, framed in pearls, was kept in a special *étui*
and was ceremoniously taken out every time the lady took a
pinch of snuff. The Duke was charmed and touched by this
little attention.

Buffon, the great naturalist, when he was dying, sent for
his snuff-box, which Madame Necker had given him with her
portrait on it, and died gazing upon her beloved features.

Though the poor man might take snuff, he was not in a
position to do so from a costly *tabatière*, but must content
himself with something simpler than would satisfy the rich
and noble collector. Here was the opportunity for commercial

enterprise to supply the demand with cheap goods. Boxes were made of lacquer, enamel and other cheap materials, and richly ornamented with miniatures. It is, in fact, the portraits on the lids which play an important part in the history of the cheap eighteenth-century snuff-box. In order to arouse the desire for the possession of new *tabatières*, the manufacturers frequently changed the subjects represented, for which the events of the day gave ample inducement.

Frederick the Great was the most popular subject for snuff-boxes in Germany during the eighteenth century. The Hohenzollern Museum owns dozens of examples of popular enamel boxes of this period. They have the king's portrait painted by hand, of course, and often scenes from his life or from stories about him; a battle, a sketch of some event such as the Peace of Hubertsburg, or the like. The jewellery and fancy goods shop of Hieronymus Löschenkohl in Vienna exhibited snuff-boxes with portraits of Austrian generals and scenes from the Turkish wars which were priced, according to the material they were made of, from one florin to six ducats each.

In 1755 Horace Walpole made presents of Battersea enamel snuff-boxes with engravings on them.

"Old Fritz" was the popular hero in Germany, and similarly in France, the rage was all for Henry IV. The worse the State finances became under the Louis, and the more confusion in the Government increased, the more passionately did men cling to memories of the first Bourbon and see in his reign a Golden Age. Therefore the portrait of his ancestor instead of himself appears on snuff-boxes during Louis XV.'s reign, and sometimes the portrait of Sully, the Finance Minister, as well. The Pompadour could think of no more delicate compliment for Laverdy, the Controller-General, than to give him a *tabatière* with a portrait of Sully on it. "See, it is a portrait of yourself," she said. After Madame Dubarry had brought about the downfall of the Duc de Choiseul, snuff-boxes with portraits of Sully on one side and the banished Duke on the other became the fashion. The malicious Sophie Arnould said, "They have income on one side and expenditure on the other."

When Louis XVI. came to the throne and people still had hopes of him, snuff-boxes appeared with Henry IV.'s portrait on one side and his on the other. In July 1774 they were selling in the Palais Royal boxes with portraits of Louis XII. and Henry IV. and the inscription, "XII. and IV. make XVI." Then appeared boxes of shagreen with portraits of the King and Queen, christened by the inventor "la consolation dans le chagrin."

After this the snuff-box portraits became more and more radical in their allusions; freemasonry, with its symbols, displaced the King's portrait and was in turn swept away by the Revolution. The Taking of the Bastille, the Declaration of the Rights of Man and the Assignats, led to portraits of all those who obtained a temporary popularity — Lafayette, Bailly, Mirabeau, Marat, Charlotte Corday, etc.

The Royalists, as well as the Republicans, had snuff-boxes with miniatures expressive of their views. There was the flight of the royal family on 20 January, 1793, for instance, and other scenes depicting the sufferings of the royal martyrs. As the possessor of one of these royalist *tabatières* was apt to find an unfortunate end to his demonstration of loyalty, it became usual to camouflage the portraits of the King and Queen, Madame Elizabeth, and the royal children. For instance, you would see an urn overhung by a weeping willow, and after close examination of its branches and leaves could at length discover the features of members of the royal family. Some years later this conceit became quite a popular game known as "Puzzle, find the cat."

The Consulate and Empire following on the Revolution bring us to Napoleon, with his family, his generals, and all the concomitants of his swift and dizzy career.

As far as the costliness of *tabatières* was concerned Napoleon carried on the tradition of the *ancien régime*. Though the boxes intended for Frenchmen generally averaged between 2400 and 3000 francs only, there was no stinginess in those destined for State and diplomatic presents. On 16 March, 1810, at Braunau, Marie Louise distributed, amongst other things, five

No. 165.   Isabey.   *Sketch for a Secretaire*

tabatières with a portrait of her husband, which had cost 46,000 francs altogether, and one of which alone was valued at 20,274 francs. The Duc de Valmy, who carried the train at the baptism of the King of Rome, received a snuff-box worth 20,000 francs for this service. Count Charles Clary, who received a miniature by Saint in 1810, which he considered "very flattering, but yet quite like," returned it immediately to the jeweller Nitot for 13,200 francs and made a journey in Switzerland on the proceeds.

Snuff-boxes were soon ordered in hundreds from jewellers, and in 1807 their prices were from 6000 to 10,000 francs. The painters who carried out portraits of the Emperor for these were Aubry, Augustin, Dumont, Gauci, Gilbert, Guérin, Isabey, Muneret, Robert Lefevre, Quaglia, Saint, Soiron, etc. They were usually paid 500 francs a miniature, Isabey alone succeeding in obtaining 600 francs for his. Many of these miniatures were in imitation of cameos in sardonyx, agatonyx or other semi-precious stones. It has already been mentioned that Napoleon was frequently displeased with the efforts to portray him, and Daru had to tell the artists to flatter him more. The goldsmith's work was mostly in the hands of Nitot et fils.

Napoleon did not take snuff himself, and Baron Meneval tells us he merely inhaled the scent of it. He paid three francs a pound, took a pinch of it between his fingers, smelt it and let it fall. This habit saved him from succumbing to a plot to kill him with poisoned tobacco that was laid at Malmaison.

He was fond of toying with a *tabatière*, and his gentlemen of the bedchamber used to keep him supplied with new ones as he mislaid or put aside those he was holding. In this way it often happened, as Las Cases relates, that he "took" far too much snuff. During the long sittings of the Council he used to borrow the snuff-boxes of the councillors, handle them and forget to return them; so finally they only brought boxes worth about fifteen sous.

For a man who did not take snuff the Emperor possessed a large number of boxes and in his will of 15 April, 1821, he left his son about forty of them, some with portraits of Peter the Great, Charles V., Turenne, etc.

Snuff-boxes with portraits on them were then still very popular gifts from important people to deserving men, and at the Vienna Congress Exhibition might be seen the magnificent boxes presented to the Duke of Wellington at the Congress. The six boxes received by Prince Trautmannsdorff were valued by Baron Schönholz at 40,000 guilders.

As snuff-taking became unfashionable, so did the custom of giving snuff-boxes as diplomatic presents. At the coronation of George IV. the ambassadors of foreign powers received snuff-boxes for which the Court jewellers were paid £8205; Moltke, who accompanied Frederick William of Prussia to London for his betrothal in 1858, wrote to his wife on the 27th January that he had spent two hours distributing six diamond-studded snuff-boxes worth 1500 to 2500 thalers.

However, Orders are distinctly cheaper, and a few inches of coloured ribbon on the coat do more credit to the wearer than the most beautiful and costly *tabatière* in his pocket. So, finally, snuff-boxes were only given to underlings as a disguised money present. The collecting of snuff-boxes remained longer in fashion than the use of snuff. Frederick William IV., who did not take snuff, had a beautiful collection which is to be seen in the Hohenzollern Museum to-day. It is curious, how-ever, that none of these contains a miniature, as though the personal application had died out with the ending of the original purpose of the snuff-box.

Amongst the numerous *tabatières* in the collection be-queathed to the Arts and Crafts Museum in Berlin by Fräulein von Uttenhoven are many costly ones in all styles and materials, but no longer any with portraits.

The eighteenth century, in which the snuff-box played such an important rôle, also had its Order of the Snuff-box. The poet Jacobi, the sentimental author of *Woldemar*, founded the Lorenzo Order of the Horn Snuff-box. In Sterne's *Senti-mental Journey*, which caused such wide-spread delight, Yorick exchanges his tortoiseshell snuff-box with the horn one of the Franciscan Lorenzo, because he wants to make up to the poor man for a previous harshness of manner towards him. In reference to this incident—well known to all *bels esprits*—the sign of the Order was a horn snuff-box with Father Lorenzo on the lid and Yorick inside. Jacobi wrote to Gleim on 4 April, 1769: "Should any of our society lose control of his temper, his friend holds out a snuff-box towards him, and this reminder is sufficient to make him restrain the strongest irritability."

Like all manners and customs which were once of importance in the higher ranks of Society, and gradually disappear from them and survive for a long time amongst a lower class (as was the case, for instance, with albums), the habit of snuff-taking went out of fashion. Good Society left off taking snuff and at the same time gave up the use of a snuff-box, whereas the middle class still retained both the habit and the box. The cheap manufactured article reproduced the popular type of snuff-box for at least half a century in the so-called Stobwasser snuff-boxes.

After the murder of Kotzebue by Charles Louis Sand, a portrait of the latter appeared on snuff-boxes; there were also represented Paganini with his Mephistophelean features and, in the eighteen-forties, Ronge the modern Luther, the founder of "German Catholicism," with sometimes the text of the famous letter to the Bishop of Trèves on the back.

In France likewise, commerce followed closely on the heels of the events of the day with its pictures for snuff-boxes, and under the Restoration, when every reminder of the glorious days of the Empire was hunted down by the childish hate of the politically-minded, some extraordinary *objets d'art* were produced.

The Bonapartists had snuff-boxes with a double lid containing a portrait of the Emperor that could be hidden from unauthorised eyes, and others which were shaped in imitation of the famous hat. After Napoleon's death, paintings of his grave at St. Helena made their appearance on the snuff-boxes of the faithful.

Liberals bought snuff-boxes from Touquet, the manufac-

No. 166. *Miniature Room in the Residence at Munich*

turer, with the text of the Charter printed on the lid; others had portraits of Rousseau or Voltaire, whose writings were widely read in opposition to the clerical-feudal *Ultras*.

In 1827 Emile Marco de Saint-Hilaire wrote concerning the political snuff-boxes:

> One ought always to carry a snuff-box with a double lid so as to have at hand a means of currying favour with persons one wishes to please and to whose political opinions one is indifferent. Three sides must be devoted to Party. The first will have the charter so cleverly devised by M. Touquet some years ago, and this will be doubtless most frequently shown. Another side will have the portrait of the ex-Emperor, which is now no longer forbidden; you need have no fear; he was a usurper I admit, but had some good qualities. Moreover, he still has friends, and a man who wants to get on in the world should neglect nobody. The third side must portray the famous banner once raised by Martainville and his friends—the white banner with the inscription "Long live the King!"

Snuff was not the only thing kept in boxes ornamented with paintings. There was a far larger number of boxes used by men and women of fashion for other things. They often had boxes with ivory tablets for making notes on, such as the little dark-green lacquered box edged with gold (p. 156) with a portrait of the Princess of Prussia on one side and her mother, the Great Landgravine of Hessen-Darmstadt (1721–1744), on the other. Like her contemporaries, Frederick, King of Prussia, and the Empress Catherine of Russia, she was called "the Great," but, unlike them, neither her fortunes nor her deeds gave sufficient justification for such a title. Perhaps it is all the more to the Landgravine's credit that she owed this description to her personality alone. It was her charm of mind which enthralled all who came into touch with her. Wieland longed to be master of Fate for one moment in order that he might make her Empress of Europe; Melchior Grimm, in a similar intoxication of enthusiasm, deplored the fact that the Princess was not almighty as Providence, for then she would be the Luck of the World. Frederick II. put on her epitaph: "A woman in body but a man in mind," and posterity has clung to Goethe's description, "the Great Landgravine."

Van Dort. *Queen Anna Katharina of Denmark and Prince Christian*

Gelton.   *Unknown Princess*

She was a Princess of Pfalzzweibrücken and lived for a long time at Prenzlau with her husband, where four of her children were born. Even after her husband came to the throne of Hessen-Darmstadt she could never get away from the narrow life of a small principality. Her correspondence made up to her (as once did Liselotte's at Versailles) for all that life denied her. She threw her whole soul into it—even to the detriment of her health—and kept up a lively interchange of ideas with all the giants of the day—Goethe, Herder, Wieland, Voltaire, etc. One of her daughters, Friederike, became the wife of Frederick William II. and Queen of Prussia; another married the Grand Prince Paul of Russia, but died before he came to the throne.

The *bonbonnière* deserves the chief place amongst boxes. These receptacles were often extremely valuable on account of the material they were made of and the art shown in beautifying them. In France the most artistic works of this kind were produced in Paris, in Germany at Augsburg, Nuremberg and Dresden, and in Italy at Naples. The Parisian jewellers Hamelin, Maillé and Drais were famous in the seventeen-fifties for the little paintings they carried out in enamel on gold boxes; they were exhibited in picture galleries for the perfection of their paintings. Amongst the subjects treated were: flowers in transparent enamel, birds, La Fontaine's *Fables*, cupids and other amorous trifles. It shows how highly they were valued when we find that Diderot in 1755 designed the scheme, carried out by Durand, of six pictures in enamel for a *tabatière*, representing a School of Love.

Costly boxes were an important part of a French princess's trousseau. The bride could not keep them herself, however, but had to distribute them amongst the ladies of her suite. Only special ones were intended for her own use; Marie Antoinette in 1770 had, amongst her wedding presents, a large octagonal gold box painted in enamel on a blue ground. It was set with 160 rose diamonds and twenty-eight brilliants and had cost 20,746 francs.

Amongst the Comtesse de Provence's wedding presents

(her husband afterwards became Louis XVIII.) was a very large box with a miniature by Blarenberghe. Amongst those of her sister-in-law the Comtesse d'Artois (whose husband became King Charles X.) there were, in 1773, boxes with miniatures after Boucher, Teniers, Watteau, etc. The most beautiful box of all, intended for the Comtesse herself, was made by the jeweller Aubert and was of gold set with 689 brilliants, 244 emeralds and 116 rubies. It cost 19,642 francs.

When the Comte du Nord (later Emperor Paul of Russia) visited Paris in 1782, Louis XVI. gave him a gold and enamel box with portraits of the King and the Empress Catherine in a wreath of twenty-four brilliants.

Louis XV.'s daughters, who led a very monotonous life at Court, were very fond of boxes of this kind. Garrand, the goldsmith, supplied Madame Christine de France in 1762 with a large oval box of gold containing a portrait of the Dauphin framed in brilliants, surrounded by medallions with the four seasons in enamel. It cost 1650 francs. The same goldsmith supplied Madame Christine with a still more costly one the same year. It was of gold and had eight portraits in enamel of Mesdames Adelaide, Victoire, Sophie and Louise, the Duke of Berry, the Counts of Provence and Artois, and Madame de France. There were 2000 diamonds round the miniatures. The price, without the diamonds, was 6800 francs.

Jacques Charlier once produced a box with twelve large miniatures each costing 1200 francs; the present cost of a similar work of art to-day, according to Henri Bouchot, would be 40,000 francs.

Madame de Genlis, in her reminiscences, speaks enthusiastically of a remarkable *bonbonnière* which the famous and mysterious Comte Saint-Germain had given her.

It is a very large box of dark tortoise-shell [she writes]. On the top it has an agate a little smaller than the lid. If you place the box in front of an open fire the agate disappears, and you see in its place a charming miniature representing a young girl holding a basket of flowers. This picture lasts until the box has got cold, and then the agate reappears.

Some smaller boxes were used to hold patches and others for the rouge which ladies carried about with them so that they could immediately rectify any faults of facial decoration. These also were adorned with miniatures, and Napoleon often had his portrait on the *étuis* containing his toothpicks. Society's rage for gambling set up a need for more boxes to contain the counters of metal or ivory with which each person was provided, so as not to use gold. For the game of *reversis* there was a special nest of four small boxes within a larger one. A Monsieur de la Vaupalière, a heavy gambler, once begged his wife for a nest of boxes. She had one made and decorated with miniatures of herself and the children with the inscription "Think of us." This pretty idea did not, unfortunately, produce the result she hoped.

The outsides and insides of note-books and pocket-books were also decorated with miniatures. In the collection of Claudius Côte, which was sold by auction in 1912, there was a beautiful pocket-book of red morocco leather lined with blue silk. It contained a miniature by Nattier, thought to represent Queen Marie Lesczynska, wife of Louis XV. If the portrait is correctly named, we behold in it the unfortunate lady whose fate it was to sit on the throne of France beside such a man as Louis XV. She was the daughter of Stanislaus Lesczynski, the Shadow-King of Poland, and if she was, as her father once said, the most boring Queen he had ever met, still she must have led a terribly empty existence at Versailles. "The loneliness here is dreadful," she wrote in 1732. "I would rather be in a convent." Her husband was quite openly unfaithful to her, and the poor woman might count herself lucky if his mistresses were polite to her, for Louis XV. himself never treated her with the least consideration.

Delbrück, the tutor of Prince William, later the Emperor William I., gave his pupil, in 1810, a beautiful pocket-book of red morocco with a portrait of himself inside.

There was great scope for the inventive faculty in the application of the miniature to various uses. The Empress Catherine of Russia had a book-marker made for her sister,

M

the Grand Duchess of Mecklenburg-Schwerin, with a blue enamel heart hanging on the end of it; when opened this displayed a miniature of the Emperor Nicholas I.

The use of miniatures for fans offers a wide field of possibilities; the two forms of art are so suitable to each other. The most famous artists have vied with one another in decking the fan with all the delicacy due to this vehicle of coquetry, and it would need a volume by itself for its history.

French princesses had to have many fans in their trousseaux, to distribute to the ladies of their suite, and every bride likewise must present the ladies of her acquaintance with a fan on her wedding-day. Paintings on fans, like those on snuff-boxes, are representative of the fashions and events of the time. Heroic under Louis XIV., piquant and frivolous under Louis XV., gallant and sentimental under Louis XVI., they then became Republican and finally Imperial.

The number of fan-painters is very great, and the productions of French artists have always been the most highly valued. The Spanish painter, Juan Cano de Arevalo, who lived in Madrid in the seventeenth century, turned this preference of his clients to his own advantage. He had painted a number of fans which he could not sell, so he spread abroad a rumour that he had received a large consignment of fans straight from Paris. In a few days he was sold out!

A fan with painting ascribed to Watteau was sold at auction in London about thirty years ago for £500.

PERSONAL BELONGINGS AND CHINA

Articles of personal use ornamented with miniature-portraits were a means of keeping the memory of the person represented ever freshly in the mind of the owner of the article.

Maria Theresa had a blotter made in 1759 for Madame de Pompadour, with a portrait of herself on it and so richly decorated with jewels that it was valued at 77,000 francs. At Chantilly there is a beautiful paper-weight of malachite

No. 167.   Schenau-Ouvrier.   *Origin of Shadow-Painting*

with a brass-gilt handle, containing a miniature of the Duchess of Aumale, who was born Princess of the Two Sicilies. A similar one with a miniature of Princess Augusta Amalia of Bavaria, painted by Franziska Schöpfer, was in the possession of King Maximilian I., and is in the National Museum at Munich.

The Archduke Rainer possesses a valuable inkstand once belonging to the Duchesse de Berry. It was made in Paris by Alfonse Giroux in 1826, and has miniature-portraits of the Duchess and her two children, her son (called later Comte de Chambord), and her daughter, the Duchess of Parma. There are also four views of the château of Rosny, the summer residence of the Duchess. Marie Louise had an inkstand of marble and brass gilt with a miniature of Queen Caroline of Naples on it.

After china was manufactured in Europe this also was added to the articles of daily household use, and finally even the poorer classes had it in place of their previous pewter and coarse earthenware. The beautiful shining white glaze seemed to ask to be painted on, and it was not long before portrait-miniatures took possession of china. The factories of Meissen, Vienna and Sèvres have achieved wonders of portraiture on porcelain, Vienna and Sèvres in particular.

In the Lanna Collection there was a cup of Old Vienna porcelain of cobalt blue decorated in gold, with a portrait of Field-Marshal Laudon, which fetched 8050 marks at auction.

Next to the fan and the snuff-box, cups were objects of especial regard. People used them, collected them, decorated the room with them; we cannot visualise the Rococo period without the snuff-box, nor the Biedermeier period (early nineteenth century) without its china. The sentimental period at the end of the eighteenth century found a useful means of expression in the china teacup; the whole superabundance of tearful sensibility was poured into it. Love and friendship, reminders of particular events and people, all found expression in pictures or writings on cup and saucer. During the Empire, porcelain articles with portraits on them were especially popular, and Napoleon made a point of giving presents of painted Sèvres china.

In 1810 Count Metternich was given a cup with a portrait of Marie Louise on a blue ground; it cost 508 francs. In 1810, the Queen of Naples was given a vase with a portrait of Napoleon that cost 1500 francs. The Comtesse de Montesquiou received in the same year a cup with a portrait of Napoleon costing 1500 francs, and the Queen of Westphalia received a cup with a portrait of the Grand Duchess of Tuscany worth 350 francs.

There were some very extravagant presents of painted china on the occasion of the baptism of the King of Rome.

The Grand Duke of Würzburg, as godfather by proxy for the Emperor of Austria, received, amongst other things, a portrait of Napoleon by Gérard de Georget painted on porcelain and worth 7000 francs; the Emperor's mother a cup with a portrait of Marie Louise, painted by Leguay after Isabey, and worth 500 francs; Queen Hortense a breakfast-service of twelve cups with pictures of the famous philosophers of antiquity painted by Bergeret and worth 3740 francs. Prince Schwarzenberg received some particularly beautiful pieces: a teapot with a portrait of Marie Louise and the Emperor of Austria worth 750 francs, and a cup with a portrait of Maria Theresa worth 400 francs.

The miniaturists who had the highest reputation for painting on Sèvres were Isabey, whose *Table des Maréchaux* has already been mentioned, Charles Etienne Leguay and Madame Jaquotot. Leguay painted, amongst other things, a breakfast-service representing on cups and saucers the joys and sorrows of love, and a large vase with thirty-three figures representing the triumphal progress of Diana. This splendid piece took three years to do and was valued at 50,000 francs. Charles X. gave it to the English ambassador, the Duke of Northumberland, at his coronation. Madame Jaquotot specialised in the painting of beautiful female heads on cups.

Dedications on china were very general in all ranks of society.

There is a whole portrait gallery of the times to be seen on cups. From kings to commoners, all sought to be immortalised on this fragile material and to express their feelings on it. Prince Biron of Courland presented his guardian Count Wassiliew, in commemoration of the end of his education, with a chocolate-service with portraits of Frederick the Great, Queen Louise and her sister.

The Goethe Museum at Weimar has a cup with his bust painted on it from the ducal china-factory in Brunswick. The factory inspector, Ludwig Sebbers, went specially to Weimar in 1826 in order to make this portrait from life. Goethe gave more than twenty sittings for the preliminary sketch and for the re-touching necessitated by it having to be fired twice. The saucer has a facsimile of Goethe's writing: "Greeting and Hail. Goethe. Weim. 28 Aug. 1826." Writing to Heinrich Meyer, the poet praises the artist for not having put in a single stroke or touch from memory, "for unquestionably he had thereby produced a very good likeness and a most praiseworthy painting."

We could easily exhibit the history of the early half of the nineteenth century in china, since we have it displayed not only on cups and other crockery, but also on pipe bowls. Snuff-taking and smoking alternated with each other, for tobacco never surrendered its lordship and only changed the form of it. The smoking of pipes, only permitted in the guard-room during the eighteenth century, begins to make its way at the beginning of the nineteenth century into the study and the inn. The short Dutch clay pipes which had been almost the only ones in use until then, gave way to the long pipe with a china bowl and so brought it to a favoured place in the hearts of all smokers. The white china bowl of the pipe was painted just as the snuff-boxes or coffee-cups were, and the heads of princes and leaders of armies which appeared on them during the Wars of Liberation gave way in due course to other heroes.

Karl Gutzkow tells us in his recollections of his youth that after the assassination of Kotzebue by Charles Louis Sand on 23 March, 1819, fifty out of every hundred smokers in Berlin had pipes with a portrait of the wretched youth on the bowl, and Fanny Lewald tells us there were as many in Königsberg. During the next ten years there followed the enthusiasm of Philhellenism, and portraits of Miaulis, Kolokotroni, Marco Bozzaris and other heroes of the Greek insurrection appeared on pipe bowls to show the sympathy of their owners for Greece. Gervinus remembered in his childhood seeing his father, who was disappointed in the Greek movement, express his displeasure publicly by having a portrait of Sultan Mahmud on his pipe, whereas all other Darmstadt citizens had the heads of Greeks on theirs.

Adermann.   *Admiral Ulric Christian Gyldenlove*

Gylding. *Augustus III, King of Poland*

In the eighteen-thirties the Greeks had to make way for new gods—the leaders of the Liberal movement in Baden, and the great speakers of the council—Itzstein, Welcker, Sander, Hoffmann—were portrayed on pipe bowls, for it was on these men that all Germans gazed in pride and hope.

History can be followed out still further on pipes from Ronge, Robert Blum and other popular men down to our own day. The true Corinthian was quite un-political and was satisfied with the head of some pretty girl on his pipe. Red cheeks, blue eyes, fair hair and a full bust pleased him more than the most heroic Greeks or the boldest orators.

The painters who had the order to do some paintings at Hohenschwangau for the Crown Prince Maximilian of Bavaria in the eighteen-thirties were helped out of an awkward situation by these pipe bowls, as Quaglio has disclosed. Moritz von Schwind had made sketches for the frescoes with which the Crown Prince wished to adorn his palace, but from economy was not allowed to undertake the carrying out of the paintings, which was handed over to younger artists who would be more modest in their charges. Now these young artists were much exercised as to how to procure models for the proud and noble ladies, the pretty citizens' daughters and the lovely nymphs, until one of them bethought himself of the pretty girls' heads on pipe bowls and beer jugs, and so saved the situation. The china beauties that look down on the beholder from the walls of the palace might well be mistaken by the majority for original von Schwinds.

The pipe bowl was as much an honourable gift as the snuff-box in its day. King Frederick VI. of Denmark gave a pipe to General von Bülow, who had taken an active part in stopping the West Indian slave-trade, in recognition of this service. It had a china bowl with a painting of the King on it, and the head of a negro on the stem.

In the days when students still smoked long pipes the gift of one with a painted bowl was very popular amongst young men.

FURNITURE

The circle of the application of the miniature is not complete without some mention of its use in the decoration of furniture —and from very early times. Ernst Lemberger mentions a table which was once in Weimar Palace and had twenty-four miniature-portraits of members of the princely house of Saxony on it, three of which had Cranach's monogram and the date 1565. The fate of this table is not known.

Seventeenth-century cabinets were often decorated with miniature-paintings. Pope Alexander VII. presented the Emperor Leopold I. in 1663 with a magnificent cabinet, the work of the cabinet-maker Hermann Müller in Rome. It is inlaid with lapis-lazuli, coloured marble and amethyst, and has paintings in gouache by Roman artists, partly scenes from Raphael's life of Constantine and partly views of Roman churches. They were fond of using a so-called "ruin-marble" for these elaborate pieces of furniture. It is a stone with veins which, at a slight distance, give an effect of antique ruins, and the artist has only to put in a few figures and trees with a fine brush to complete the illusion of a picture. The Kurfürstin Anna of Saxony had a work-table entirely inlaid with "ruin-marble." The Vienna Hofmuseum possesses a portable altar of ebony with enamel and silver ornaments and a marble slab in which the natural markings of the stone are used to make a picture of the Annunciation. In an ante-room of King William's palace at Berlin there is an ebony table with the top inlaid with plates of "ruin-marble."

In the eighteenth century, when fashion in furniture under Louis XVI. drew upon all the elements of decoration, people used painted porcelain plaques, medallions of *eglomisé* and other techniques of miniature-painting with which to inlay cabinets. The most striking example of this piling up of decorative material is the jewel cabinet of Marie Antoinette, with the brasswork by Thomire and miniatures by Degault. The cabinet-maker David Röntgen of Neuwied, who made richly inlaid writing-tables of great magnificence at the end of the eighteenth century, also made use of miniature-portraits. In the Hohenzollern Museum is a secretaire belonging to Frederick William II. with a portrait of the King on ivory let into it. Queen Louise possessed a large casket with miniature-portraits on the panels, and at the Palazzo Favorite at Palermo is still to be seen a beautiful table that once belonged to Queen Caroline of Naples. It is of mahogany inlaid with narrow strips of bronze, and five miniatures of members of the royal family are let in on the top.

The sumptuous pieces of furniture with miniatures by Isabey have already been mentioned. At the Mannheim exhibition of miniatures were to be seen settees ornamented with miniatures, and there were particularly numerous and beautiful pieces of furniture decorated with miniatures at the Vienna Congress Exhibition; there were gentlemen's and ladies' writing-tables with miniatures on the doors and flaps, an ebony and morocco leather work-table with very small water-colour miniatures, and many more. Countess Boigne saw a mirror belonging to the Duchesse de Chatillon with portraits of her numerous lovers let into the frame. At the K. K. Austrian Museum at Stubenring is a lady's work-table of Hungarian ash inlaid with polished steel and with four miniatures by Wiegand on the flaps; also a mahogany writing-table by Stoll inset with miniatures. The lacquer-work of Stobwasser was much used for painting on furniture; a mahogany secretaire in the Bier Bequest at the Berlin Arts and Crafts Museum is one of the finest specimens of furniture of the Biedermeier period and has two inner doors painted in this technique with Swiss landscapes.

INTERIOR DECORATION

The art of miniature-painting seems, on account of its intimate effect, to be naturally debarred from serving as room decoration, but people were once of a different opinion. Queen Catherine de Médicis had a room in her palace at Paris with seventy-one Limoges enamel paintings let into the panelling of the walls. At the Favorite Palace, which the Margravine Sibylle had built at Baden-Baden at the beginning of the eighteenth century, there were two salons decorated in this manner. In the "Mirror Room" there were seventy-two portraits of the Margravine's family painted in water-colour on vellum in "Indian frames." Amongst these the builder of the palace was depicted more than a dozen times and in all possible costumes—as Diana, a Bacchante, Spaniard, Persian, Swiss, Slav, etc. In the "Florentine Room" there were 150 miniatures on ivory under glass, portraits of painters after the engravings in Sandrart's *Academia Tedesca* (German Academy).

Prince Eugene of Savoy had a room arranged in the Belvedere at Vienna,

on the walls of which could be seen the most costly and beautiful miniature-paintings, which are said to have cost 200,000 florins altogether, and separate items as much as twenty, thirty and fifty thousand florins apiece. All the paintings were in broad gilt frames with a pattern of flowers.

The Margravine Wilhelmina of Bayreuth expresses herself as enraptured with the writing-room of her husband at the Hermitage, the walls of which were covered with plaques of Viennese porcelain with miniatures on them.

The Bavarian Electoral Prince Max III. had a whole room decorated with miniatures by Joseph Bucher.

After passing through the state-rooms of the Residence at Munich we come at last to a small writing-room which was decorated by François Cuvilliés (p. 165). The ceiling is white with gilded ornaments of the year 1733 by Zimmermann, the carved and gilded woodwork on a ground of red lacquer of the walls and doors was by Joachim Dietrich, 1732. In the framework of rococo ornamentation on the walls are 128 miniature-paintings. They are copies of the masterpieces of famous German, Italian and Dutch painters.

This kind of miniature-copy of a famous painting gave great pleasure to many people though it was far from being a slavish copy of the original.

When the Duchess Sophia of Hanover visited Duke Wolf-gang Wilhelm of the Palatinate at Düsseldorf she admired the decoration of his bedroom, on the walls of which scenes from the Old and New Testaments were represented in more than 100 miniatures.

The Archduke Ferdinand of the Tyrol had brought together at the Palace of Ambras hundreds of miniature-portraits of the past and present.

The Empress Eleanora Magdalena Theresa presented her husband, the Emperor Leopold I., on his birthday with a portable altar in the form of a monstrance containing a miniature of the Nativity after Dürer under crystal.

David Teniers (1610–1690), who was Court painter in Brussels and one of the Directors of the Archduke Leopold William's Gallery, frequently painted the collection in minia-ture. He has done four moderate-sized paintings representing the walls of the gallery with the pictures on them, and they are so faithful and exact that we can identify each picture; therefore these paintings of Teniers are of great help in the researches of the historian of art. Teniers' originals are at the Old Pinakothek at Munich, and the collection he depicted was transferred to the Belvedere and thence to the Vienna Hofmuseum.

Teniers copied the paintings in the collection of the Arch-duke Leopold a second time in order to have engravings made from them. A part of this collection—about 120 miniatures— came into the possession of the Duke of Marlborough and fetched £2002 at the Blenheim Palace sale.

In the eighteenth century Baron von Brabeck, who had a famous picture gallery at Söder, had the best pictures from it copied in miniature by Johann Christian Kuntze of Bonn, in order that he could take the copies with him when he went travelling, and so not miss his collection so much.

Teniers' method of copying the Archduke's collection in one moderate-sized picture had many imitators, and Theodor von Frimmel has brought all this material together in his work on painted galleries.

THE SILHOUETTE

No. 168.   Johann Rud. Schellenberg.   *Silhouette Machine*

THE SILHOUETTE

THE art of the miniature had, up to the eighteenth century, numerous exponents and various techniques, but there was as yet no mechanical means of producing a portrait absolutely true to life.

The artist who painted or drew was always between the original and the portrait, and the likeness depended upon his eye or hand.

The silhouette did not appear until the second half of the eighteenth century, and though it was not a complete portrait, it gave a very characteristic outline of the profile, and that in a sufficiently mechanical way to be attempted by people other than artists.

The silhouette has a twofold origin.

G. Jacob has proved its existence in mediæval Persia and drawn attention to some of her productions—mostly Persian texts with painted borders—which are to be seen in German libraries. In the sixteenth century there was a guild of professional silhouette-cutters at Constantinople. The oldest German silhouettes known at present are certainly founded on an acquaintance with this Oriental art. There is a leaf from an album of a certain Johann David Schäffer of Tübingen, dated 1631, and a series of twenty-eight portraits by a certain R. V. Hus (or, as some spell it, Hut or Hess), of the years 1653–1654. They are cut out with scissors in white paper and laid on coloured paper. In the seventeenth and eighteenth centuries a great number of leaflets of this sort were produced in convents, mostly a central figure of the Virgin or Saints with an ornamental border. A particularly good, that is to say elaborate, example of a small work of this kind is an Ex-Voto of 1708 in the museum at Linz. The National Museum

183

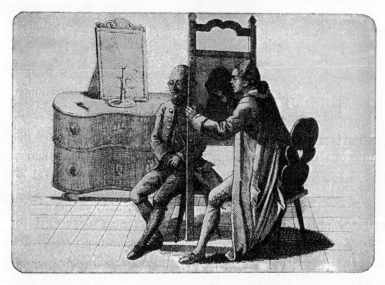

No. 169. Shadowgraph Artist. *Engraving from Lavater's "Physiognomy"*

at Munich has an example of silhouette work by G. M. Kellner, 1746, representing a stag hunt. In this an attempt at effects of perspective is made by placing one sheet over another. The shadow-picture, too, has its origin in the East and goes back to the shadow-theatre of the Far East, of China and Java. Paul Kahle found, during his excavations in the Nile Valley, the puppets of an Islamitic shadow-theatre of early mediæval times. In 1700 there was a shadow-theatre at Hamburg, in which marionettes played. Perhaps they came to London from the Hansa town; at anyrate the first portrait silhouettes appeared in England.

In 1699 a paper-cutting woman artist called Pyburg cut out heads of William III. and Queen Mary in black paper, and the verses of Swift (*d.* 1745) on *Silhouettes* show that this practice had not fallen into disuse. In a letter to Sir Horace Mann in 1761 Horace Walpole thanks him for sending a silhouette of the Duchess of Grafton, which had been made by a famous paper-cutter of Geneva. This letter of the well-known English art-patron brings us up to the time when the

Müller. *Professor Pedcrals*

Müller. *Professor J. Wiedewelt*

silhouette had suddenly become the fashion. Whatever its origin and however it was produced before this time, its importance and even its name date from the end of the eighteenth century.

Etienne de Silhouette (1709–1767), one of the Pompadour's protégés, was made in 1759 Controller-General of Finances or Finance Minister, and was at first very popular, for he commenced with economies in the royal household. His popularity only lasted until the fund-holders, pensioners and others began to feel the pinch in their own purses. Then popularity turned to hate and Monsieur de Silhouette was forced to give up his thankless task after barely eight months. The quizzical Parisians, while he was still in office, had given all kinds of fashionable knick-knacks and hobbies the name of this minister they so suddenly hated, to make him ridiculous, and thus the shadow-picture, for which M. de Silhouette had a liking, received its name, according to Sebastian Mercier, a writer of the day. In 1759 he built himself a château at Brie on the Marne, several rooms of which were decorated with silhouettes which he made himself.

No. 170. *Goethe*

The silhouette, as the shadow-picture was from henceforth called, quickly gained popularity. In 1760 the Landgravine Caroline of Hesse sent one to Princess Amalia, and wrote: "They say necessity begets invention, so these are named silhouettes after their parent."

Several things worked together to produce an almost sensational success for the silhouette. It needs no training and is easy to do, and very charming if sharply cut and a good likeness. Added to all this was the enthusiasm of the day for classical antiquity. Lichtwark was the first to point out the resemblance between the silhouette and the black figures on

N

the vases which were just then being found in hundreds in the burial-grounds of South and Middle Italy, and which were much admired and eagerly collected. In the silhouette there lay a cheap and easy means of becoming a master of classical taste. Lastly comes, in Germany at any rate, the cult of physiognomy which had been popularised by Lavater of Zürich. In his *Fragments of Physiognomy for the Furtherance of Human Knowledge and Love*, which appeared between 1775 and 1778, he tries to lay the foundations of the knowledge of the human soul in the features and formation of the head and, since he cannot dispense with illustration, uses portraits or, for preference, silhouettes. He says in the eleventh Fragment of the second volume:

No. 171. *Goethe*

The silhouette is the emptiest and weakest representation of a man, but at the same time, if a light is put at some distance and the face throws its shadow on to a plain background you can produce the most faithful portrait a man can have. Weak, for it is negative and not positive, only the outline of half the face; faithful because it is a direct transcript from Nature, such as not even the most gifted artist could do freehand. No art [he continues farther on] approaches a well-made silhouette in truth. I have collected more physiognomical information from silhouettes than from all other portraits, and sharpened my sense of character more on them than even by observing ever-changing Nature herself. The silhouette draws one's scattered observation together and concentrates it on outline only and so makes one's observation simpler and more distinct, and with it the power of comparison. Physiognomy has no more irrefutable proof of its objective truth than the silhouette.

No. 172. *Goethe with Fritz von Stein*

One can imagine the effect of such a statement on human vanity. Lavater, who would gladly have called in the whole world to work with him, was inundated with silhouettes from all parts of Germany. People sent their silhouettes to the physiognomist of Zürich always in the expectation of hearing something very interesting and important — just as they send up their handwriting to have their characters told nowadays (a task Lavater also undertook in his *Fragments*). Since Lavater printed numerous silhouettes in his great work and added commentaries on them which seem peculiar to-day in their exuberance, there was always the hope of seeing one's self portrayed in such a famous and widely-read book. Caroline von Greiner, the mother of Caroline Pichler, corresponded with Lavater about her silhouette, and when Lavater, accompanied by his draughtsman Schmoll, had the Goethe family sketched and silhouetted at Frankfurt-on-Main,

on 23 June, 1774, "Frau Aja" was delighted at the prospect of seeing her portrait in the famous book. Meanwhile Goethe begged his friend at Zürich not to publish the profile of his mother, and so she had the great disappointment of finding her husband's portrait without hers published in the next volume. She did not get over this disappointment for a long time.

Lavater's example spread all over the kingdom. In 1775 Biester wrote from Bützow to Bürger that there was "a rage for silhouettes," and Lichtenberg wrote from Hanover about the "physiognomical frenzy" there.

Goethe took up Lavater's theories of physiognomy with great enthusiasm, and went in for silhouette-cutting as an amusement himself. Physiognomy and silhouettes play a great part

No. 173.   *Frau von Stein holding Bust Portrait of her Son*

in his letters, not only to Lavater, but also to Kestner, his brother-in-law Schlosser, Jacobi, Countess Augusta Stolberg, Merck and other friends. His observations on the silhouette of Frau von Stein, which Zimmermann showed him at Strasburg before he met her, show how convinced he was of the correctness of Lavater's theory: "It would be a wonderful thing to see the world mirrored in this soul, which sees the world as it is and yet through the medium of love. Gentleness is the general impression she gives." Goethe still kept his liking for the silhouette after he had abandoned Lavater's theories. In 1792 he writes from Champagne: "Everyone was a practised silhouettist, and no stranger could pass without having his shadow thrown on the wall; the pantograph was never at rest." Even in his old age he favoured and himself practised

No. 174. *Cornelia Schlosser*

the art of the silhouette; for instance, he put together an album of personalities of Court Society for Marianne von Willemer.

Early German silhouettes have a particular interest, as there are so many characteristic portraits associated with the

No. 175. *Schiller*

great eighteenth-century poets. The full-length pictures of Goethe alone (pp. 185, 186), or in company with his pupil Fritz von Stein (p. 187), show the poet as the stiff Frankfurt burgher's son he appeared in those days to Weimar Society according to the former Court page, Lyncker. The pendant of Frau von Stein holding the bust of her son (p. 188) is very characteristic of the fashion of the day both in hair and dress. Fritz von Stein, who appears in these silhouettes, was the youngest son of Goethe's friend Charlotte von

Schardt and her husband Baron von Stein, Master of the Horse.
He is an example of the slight power of education over natural
tendencies. Goethe's pupil, to whom he had devoted all the
love and care of his rich nature, became a dusty bureaucrat
who turned his back on Weimar at the first opportunity, and
took service under Prussia. He was born in 1772 and lived
in Goethe's house from 1783 to 1786; he lived with Schiller in
1791, while he was studying at the University of Jena, and
associated during the years of his youth with all the great
minds of Germany at her most brilliant period. Körner, who
met him in Dresden in 1795, was greatly disappointed in
him, and thought him lacking in any signs of capability.
"Such men as he," was Schiller's reply to him from Jena
on 16 November, 1795, "can only maintain the world as
it is, and not advance it a step." Fritz von Stein was lucky
enough to become a Prussian Regierungsrat in Silesia in
1797 instead of having to take the post offered him of tutor
to the Crown Prince. He settled down in this province and in
1810 became General Provincial Representative of Silesia.
He married twice, but both marriages were unhappy. His
first wife was Helena Baroness von Stosch.

Goethe's sister Cornelia (p. 189) has hidden the peculiar
shape of her forehead under a large hat. Goethe has given
an arresting description of his sister in *Wahrheit und Dichtung*
(Truth and Fiction). He writes there:

She was tall, but well and delicately built, and had a natural dignity
of bearing that merged into a pleasing gentleness. Her features, neither
striking nor beautiful, spoke of a spirit that was not at one with itself
and never could be. Her eyes, though not the most beautiful I have
ever seen, yet had depths which made one expect great things, and
which lighted up wonderfully to express affection or love. Yet their
expression was not exactly tender like that which comes from the heart,
and has something of longing and desire in it. Their expression came
from the soul, and was rich and full, only wanting to give and never
to receive. But what quite spoilt her face, so that she sometimes looked
really ugly, was the fashion of the day which exposed the whole forehead, and not only that, but did everything to make it apparently,
or in fact, higher. As she had a most feminine rounded forehead, heavy
black eyebrows, and prominent eyes, this circumstance produced a

contrast which certainly did not attract, if it did not actually repel, anyone on first seeing her. She was aware of this from a very early age, and became more and more sensitive to it as she approached the age when both sexes begin to take an innocent pleasure in each other's society. No one can dislike his own person, the ugliest of us has as much right as the most beautiful to rejoice in his appearance, and since good-will is a beautifier and everyone looks at themselves benevolently in the glass, we can truly say that everyone must behold himself with satisfaction even if he strives against it. Although my sister was unusually intelligent, she was incredibly blind and stupid in this matter. She knew to her sorrow that she was far below her companions in outward beauty, without taking comfort from the fact that she was far above them in beauty of mind and spirit. Indeed, if her appearance was to some extent discouraging, her spirit shone through without being able to attract, for each virtue in turn threw the next into the shade.

Cornelia Goethe was married on 1 November, 1773, to Johann Georg Schlosser, and after continual ill-health died on 24 September, 1777. Two years later the widower married Johanna Fahlmer, a friend of Goethe's, who had corresponded charmingly with the poet.

No. 176. *Charlotte von Schiller*

The silhouette of Schiller (p. 189) is the earliest known portrait of the poet. It was probably done about 1772 and was amongst the effects of his sister Christophine Reinwald. His wife (p. 191), Charlotte von Schiller (*née* von Lengefeld), was born in 1766, married to him in 1790, became a widow in 1805, and died at Bonn in 1825, twenty-one years after her famous husband.

The Duchesses Anna Amalia (1739–1807) and Louise (1757–1830) of Sachsen-Weimar (p. 192) were the queens of the little Court of the Muses on the Ilm. Anna Amalia had to be regent for her infant son in 1758 while herself a minor.

Charlotte Kestner (p. 193) is the original of Werther's Lotte. She was born Charlotte Buff in 1753 and died in 1828.

Joachim Heinrich Campe (p. 194), the famous pedagogue

No. 177.   *The two Duchesses of Weimar*

(1746–1818), would have remained unknown outside his own sphere had he not introduced us to *Robinson the Younger*. This work was a trial of patience to the young on account of the extremely silly interpolated questions ("Father, what is a coach?"), but it lasted from its first appearance in 1779 till 1864, and passed through sixty-seven editions.

One of the earliest silhouettes is of the Margravine Friederike Caroline of Ansbach (1735–1791); (p. 205). She was a princess of Sachsen-Saalfeld and married the Margrave Alexander of Ansbach, who was a year younger than herself, in 1754. The marriage was not happy, in spite, or perhaps because of, the efforts of the famous French *tragédienne* Clairon, the Margrave's friend, to reconcile them. Scarcely was the Margravine dead when the widower renounced his throne, handed his lands over to Prussia and in the same year married another of his friends, Elizabeth Berkeley, widow of Lord Craven. He went to live in England with her, but although he procured her the title of Princess of Berkeley in 1801, he could not get good Society to accept her. She entertained a great deal at Brandenburg House and Benham Valence, but her circle was not quite of the best Society, who could not forget the many years of unmarried relationship of the "Margravine," as they called her.

If the fashionable craze for silhouettes could appeal to a man like Goethe we can easily imagine what a huge circle of ordinary people it would attract. Silhouettes were collected and exchanged as stamps are to-day. Since the interest in the Biedermeier period drew attention to the silhouette, and its history has been treated by Leisching, E. Nevil Jackson and others, a great quantity of eighteenth-century collections of silhouettes has been brought to light. Ernst Kroker published the collection of Georg Friedrich Ayrer, a councillor of Schönberg; Hans Knudsen that of Wilhelm Christian Dietrich Meyer, who was director of the theatre at Mannheim. Paul Zimmermann published the collection of J. A. Leisewitz; Leo Grünstein brought out the silhouette collection left by Johann Heinrich Merck at Darmstadt; and Theodor Kroeber found numbers

No. 178. *Charlotte Kestner*

of valuable silhouettes of the best period in Weimar and Gotha. Numerous exhibitions at Berlin, Brünn, Danzig and Düsseldorf showed that the silhouette, either drawn or cut, is more than a game and can almost be considered as an art.

These collections give a good idea of how the taste for the silhouette increased. Out of the 1370 items put together by Councillor Ayrer only a few date from the years 1764–1767, whilst the greater number date from 1768–1779. The year 1780 marks the height of the fashion, for in this and the previous year three hand-books appeared simultaneously at Münster, Leipzig and Frankfurt-on-Main, giving information on the art of drawing silhouettes. In 1778 young Ayrer made the silhouette known to Lausanne society. About the same time the people of Hamburg took it up, and in 1780, Johann Schopenhauer tells us in his reminiscences, the art of the silhouette was in full swing at Danzig.

Although all ranks of Society pursued the art of the silhouette as a fashionable hobby, there were also numbers of artists who depended on it for a living. The year 1780 is also a turning-point in this respect. Leisching has shown that Meusel's *Dictionary of Artists* mentions no single silhouettist in the edition of 1778, but the 1789 edition contains the names of several. These are: C. D. Henning and Andreas Leonhard Möglich of Nuremberg, Ernst Valentini of Detmold, Bernhard Rode and G. J. Burmester in Berlin, Johann Gottlieb Solbrig and Johann Adolf Opitz of Dresden. The last-named even had some of his silhouettes exhibited at the Academy.

No. 179. *Campe*

Round about the year 1800, a certain Näther made a living by travelling between Leipzig, Halle, Magdeburg, Halberstadt, Dresden, Bautzen, Zittau and Görlitz making silhouettes.

Johann Friedrich Anthing of Gotha travelled all over Europe between 1783 and 1800 and published a collection of 100 engravings from his own silhouettes. This work has become so rare that it has been reprinted by Professor Schüddekopf for the Society of Bibliophiles.

Just as the masters of miniature art had their own techniques and styles, the silhouettists had their own special apparatus. Leonhard Heinrich Hessel of Petersburg (born 1757) worked in Nuremberg and invented a machine called Hessel's cutter, that could be used by daylight.

Ernst Christian Specht of Gotha made himself an affair
of glass for the same purpose. Jakob von Döhren had an

No. 180. *Queen Louise at the Writing-Table*

invention he called "boumagie," that is, a means of reproducing silhouettes.

In the illustration from Lavater's *Physiognomy* (p. 184)
we see a silhouettist at work with his machine.

No. 181. *Mother and Daughter.* By Schüttner, 1843

In Vienna, Löschenkohl, the bookseller, had a veritable silhouette-factory. His activity was such that he is said to have published silhouettes of the members of an embassy from Morocco before they had been seen by anyone.

At first silhouettists only attempted to reproduce a profile of the bust in solid black; then they went farther and cut out whole figures. Numbers of these have been preserved. They needed great care in the cutting to bring out all the little details of figure, toilet and even furniture correctly, as we see from the silhouette of Queen Louise at her writing-table (p. 195).

To this class of silhouette belongs also the picture of Friedrich Wilhelm II. and the rest of the Prussian Royal Family (p. 202). On the right is the King (1741–1797), on the left the Queen Friederike, born Princess of Hessen-Darmstadt. She was married in 1769, a few months after the King (then Prince of Prussia) had divorced his first wife. She only survived him eight years. His divorced wife Elizabeth, Princess of Brunswick, lived until 1840 at Stettin in the castle where she was kept more or less a prisoner. The eldest daughter, Friederike (1727–1810), became Duchess of York in 1791 and was partly responsible for the fashion of short waists, for

Hoyer.   *Queen Maria Sophia Frederica of Denmark*

Hornemann. *Self Portrait*

No. 182   *The Poet Matthison before his Royal Master.*
Silhouette by Christiane Duttenhofer

when her figure altered with circumstances, the English ladies padded themselves in front under their girdles so as to look like their beloved Princess. The second daughter, Wilhelmine (1774–1837), married Prince William of the Netherlands, who became the first King of the Netherlands by decision of the Vienna Congress, under the name of William I., and after the death of his wife married again in spite of his great age. He renounced his throne and married Countess Henriette d'Oultremont (whom he made Countess Nassau) in 1841. To the great scandal of Berlin Court Society the happy pair lived in the palace in the Wilhelmstrasse that belonged to Prince Albrecht, the King's son-in-law. The third daughter, Augusta (1780–1841), was unfortunate enough to marry Prince Wilhelm of· Hessen-Cassel, who became so notorious as the Elector Wilhelm II. No fear of the Berlin Court prevented him from treating his wife abominably. It was in the interests of this much-to-be-pitied Princess that Varnhagen von Ense made a journey to Cassel, the last diplomatic mission entrusted to this always dissatisfied diarist. The eldest son of the King, the Crown Prince, ascended the Prussian throne as Friedrich Wilhelm III.

Next to him stands his brother Ludwig (1773–1796). Both brothers married, in 1793, the beautiful Mecklenburg sisters, the Crown Prince Princess Louise, and Ludwig Princess Friederike, who married twice after his death, first the Prince Frederick William of Solms-Braunfels and then Duke Ernest Augustus of Cumberland, who became King of Hanover. The younger sons who are still children in this silhouette are Prince Heinrich (1781–1846) and Prince Wilhelm (1783–1851). The elder boy became a Grand Master of the Order of St. John and lived for years at Rome; Moltke was his adjutant and found leisure, while in this post, to make a map of the Campagna. Prince Wilhelm, called "brother" to distinguish him from Prince Wilhelm "son," later Kaiser Wilhelm I.,

No. 183.   *Uhland.*   By Christiane Duttenhofer

married Princess Marianne of Hessen-Homburg (1785–1846), a very charming lady, who plays a great rôle in letters and memoirs of the day.

Silhouette artists went a step farther and began to touch in the accessories of hair, clothing and jewellery in Chinese white, and finally to put together pictures with several figures in them. This must be considered an error of taste. Löschenkohl of Vienna showed representations of the Last Hours of

Maria Theresa, Promenading on the Prater, etc., in which the details of locality and the dresses of the persons represented were given with great exactitude, whilst the heads were all in black profile. This style became very popular for family groups.

The silhouette illustrated on p. 203 represents Borussia's Grief at the Tomb of Prince Frederick Louis Charles. He was the second son of King Friedrich Wilhelm II. of Prussia, and died in 1796 when only twenty-three years old. This paper memorial cannot have caused the artist as much vexation as did the marble monument ordered by the widow of Schadow, which could never be finished.

The plain black and white of the original silhouette gave way to more and more variations as long as the fashion lasted. Sometimes the

No. 184.   *Therese Huber the Editress.*
By Christiane Duttenhofer

black cutting would be laid on a background of gold, or different colours; the tones were changed over so that white silhouettes were sometimes laid on a black ground. One of these inverted silhouettes, as one might call them, is the portrait of Lord Byron (p. 200), cut by Mrs. Leigh Hunt between January and June 1822, only two years before his death. He was living at that time with the beautiful Countess Teresa Guiccioli at Pisa. Whilst there he lost his friend Shelley, who was drowned whilst sailing between Livorno and Lerici.

No. 185.　*Lord Byron*

Byron arranged a funeral ceremony that caused a great sensation at the time. He had his friend's body burned on a funeral pyre on the sea-shore and the ashes placed on the pyramid of Cestius at Rome. The traveller to-day will find there a memorial to the friendship of both poets.

The clear silhouette was much used as a basis for various conceits. A figure would be introduced into the contours of the black and white which had nothing whatever to do with the actual picture and took some trouble to find. During the Reign of Terror one might see snuff-boxes for sale in Paris with representations of a weeping willow over a grave. On closer inspection white silhouettes of the guillotined King and Queen and their children could be discovered in the branches of the tree. Later on the same thing was done with portraits of the *petit caporal*.

These refinements of technique disfigured the true character of the silhouette and foreboded the decay of this form of art.

The best period of the silhouette in Germany was during the last thirty years of the eighteenth century; after the beginning of the nineteenth it disappeared from good Society and remained for some time popular with the middle classes and the students. In this period also artists made use of the silhouette technique, but there are only one or two solitary instances of this. Otto Philip Runge of Hamburg was a clever silhouettist with whose plant studies Goethe, who made his acquaintance in 1806, was enchanted and immediately wanted to have a room papered with them. Lichtwark has collected and published these. At the same time there lived at Stuttgart a woman silhouette-artist whom Pazaurek has rescued from an undeserved oblivion. Christiane Louise Duttenhofer, *née* Hummel (1776–1829), handled the scissors with truly marvellous ability; grace and beauty, deliberate mockery or biting satire, all were at her command. How maliciously she represents Friedrich von Matthison

No. 186. *Unknown Lady of* 1830

(1761–1831), the *poète larmoyant*, behind whose sentimental lyricism one would never have suspected the Court sycophant she suggests (p. 197). But what might not a poet do to be, like Matthison, in rapid succession ennobled, made privy councillor, manager of the royal theatre and head librarian?

The young Uhland (1787–1862; p. 198) provides a very strong contrast to him. On the one hand the Court toady, on the other the stiff-necked non-conformer, for whom the greatest thing in the world was "age-old right and justice."

Frau Duttenhofer has characterised Therese Huber (p. 199) as subtly as these two. She has portrayed the famous lady at the time when she was editing an influential morning

o

No. 187.   *Frederick William II. and his Family*

paper for Cotta and thereby brought upon herself vexatious quarrels with, amongst others, Müllner the author of the *Schuld*. She was born in 1764 and was the daughter of the famous philologist Heyne of Göttingen, and married the unstable, restless Johann Georg Forster in 1784. In 1794 she became the wife of L. F. Huber, with whom she had a short but happy married life. She died in 1829.

Next to Frau Duttenhofer the most gifted silhouettists of this period are Varnhagen von Ense and Adela Schopenhauer, the sister of the philosopher. Varnhagen was famous for his skill in cutting silhouettes even before his marriage to his famous wife. Adela Schopenhauer, who wrote such charming books, frequently had verses written to her by Goethe expressing his admiration for her skill with silhouettes.

Germany is the true home of the silhouette. Neither in France, whence it received its name, nor in England, where

No. 188. *Borussia's Grief at the Tomb of Prince Friedrich Ludwig Carl*

it received its first impetus, did it attain the same widespread popularity as on the other side of the Rhine.

In France it hardly achieved any importance at all. In Grimm's correspondence in 1772 there is mention of a certain famous silhouettist named Huber, but he was a Swiss protégé of Voltaire's. The only known French silhouette-artist, François Gonord, was unable to earn a living in Paris and travelled to London and Vienna to seek his fortune. In 1788 he lived at the Palais Royal and made silhouettes for people at prices varying from twenty-four sous to seventy-five francs; silhouettes *à l'anglaise*, that is, with dress and hair painted in, cost 120 francs; coloured silhouettes 250 francs.

Another French silhouettist, Auguste Edouart, also left his home and settled in England, where he made a speciality of portraits made out of hair.

Madame de Genlis, famous as a novelist and as governess to the Duke of Orleans' family, also tried her skill at silhouette-cutting and was certainly very pleased with the results herself, for she showed some of her performances to the Countess

No. 189. *Writing-Table of Queen Louise.* Hohenzollern Museum.
Schloss Monbijou

No. 190. *Music in the Home.* Silhouette by Moritz von Schwind for Schloss Rüdigsdorf near Altenburg, 1838

Apponyi with the remark, "Have you ever seen anything so perfect?"

Jackson mentions John Miers of Leeds and A. Charles of London as eighteenth-century English silhouettists whose portraits fetched from 2s. 6d. to £44. A Mr. Edward Beetham invented a machine for diminishing the silhouette to the required size, and M. Tussaud, the son of Madame Tussaud, whose wax-works were famous throughout the world at the beginning of the nineteenth century, invented a machine for silhouette-cutting. His portraits cost from two to seven shillings.

With regard to technique, the silhouette contains almost unlimited possibilities of reproduction, whilst the miniature developed in the direction of painting pure and simple. The silhouette was cut out, painted, drawn, engraved on copper, printed on banners, fans and in books, painted on china, enamel, *eglomisé*, cut on glass; in a word, nothing was left undone to lend it charm and use it for adornment. The silhouette does not lag behind the miniature in the many uses to which it was put. It was just as much worn in medallions and rings.

No. 191. *The Margravine Friederike Caroline von Ansbach*

When Frau Rath Weinachten sent a medallion containing her silhouette-portrait

No. 192. *Josefa Rollett, née Trost.*
By Moritz von Schwind for
Dr. Rollett's summer-house at
Baden, near Vienna, 1841

to Fräulein von Göchhausen at Weimar in 1785, the latter thanked her enthusiastically, saying that the whole Court envied her this trinket.

The various china-factories speedily took possession of the silhouette. In Vienna vases were decorated with silhouettes in imitation of the black figures on the Greek amphoræ, and there is Ludwigsburg porcelain with black borders from sketches by Frau Duttenhofer, Worcester china with silhouettes of English kings, Sèvres cups with portraits of Mirabeau. Frederick William II. had a coffee-service made for use at his favourite castle on Pfau Island, each piece of which had a silhouette-portrait of some member of the royal family. Amongst Frederick the Great's effects there was a golden *étui* with a silhouette of the Duchess of Brunswick on white enamel. Silhouettes are met with on the numerous boxes and pipe heads produced commercially.

Queen Louise had a small writing-table of the kind called "bonheur du jour," with a silhouette on it (p. 204). At the Württemberg smelting works at Wasseralfingen two artists, G. K. Weitbrecht (1796–1836) and his pupil Christian Plock (1809–1882), made relief figures after the style of a silhouette in cast-iron for the decoration of furniture, buildings and household effects. There are numbers of new casts from the old moulds reproduced by A. Wertheim in Berlin.

Moritz von Schwind, that amiable master, was well acquainted with the silhouette art and used it for the decoration of whole rooms. For the castle of Dr. Crusius at Rüdigsdorf, near Altenburg, he painted a frieze of sil-

Hornemann. *Christian VIII of Denmark*

houettes in red wash in 1838, that is most striking in its beauty. The vivacity and grace of the figures have all the charm of a truly startling naturalness. Even more artistically successful are the friezes with which he decorated the summer-house of Dr. Karl Rollett in Baden, near Vienna, in 1841. They consist of twenty-eight figures in four series, one on each wall; the material used is coloured wrapping-paper. It has that intimate enchantment that breathes from everything that came from Moritz von Schwind's hands (pp. 206, 207).

Seraphim Dominique François opened a shadow-theatre in 1771 in Paris and called it *théâtre Seraphin*. In Germany Count Pocci and Clemens Brentano wrote little plays for the *ombres chinoises*, and to-day the cinema has adopted the idea, and shadow-dramas may be seen on the films.

The painter and engraver Kennedy (called Quénédey in France) (1756–1830) made use of the silhouette principle for portraits by improving Chrétien's apparatus, the "Physionotrace," and by its means produced mechanically thousands of portraits.

No. 193. *Lady of the Rollett Circle.* By Moritz von Schwind for Dr. Rollett's summer-house at Baden

No. 194. *Hunting Scene*

INDEX OF ARTISTS AND SITTERS

INDEX OF ARTISTS AND SITTERS